Relationship, Relationship, Relationship

Other Titles by Tony Humphreys
Self-Esteem, the Key to your Child's Future
Leaving the Nest
The Power of 'Negative' Thinking
Myself, my Partner
Worth & Worth, Take back your Life
A Different Kind of Teacher
A Different Kind of Discipline
Whose Life are you Living?
The Mature Manager
All About Children: Questions Parents Ask

Also by Tony Humphreys and Helen Ruddle
The Compassionate Intentions of Illness

Book Titles with Helen Ruddle
O'Connor, J., Ruddle, H., and O'Gallagher, M., *Caring for the Elderly, Part II: The Caring Process: A Study of Carers in the Home*
O'Connor, J., Ruddle, H., and O'Gallagher, M., *Cherished Equally? Educational and Behavioural Adjustment of Children*
O'Connor, J., and Ruddle, H., *You Can Do It: A Life Skills Book for Women*
O'Connor, J., Ruddle, H., and O'Gallagher, M., *Sheltered Housing in Ireland: Its Role and Contribution in the Care of the Elderly*
O'Connor, J., and Ruddle, H., *Business Matters for Women*
O'Connor, J., and Ruddle, H., *Breaking the Silence, Violence in the Home: The Woman's Perspective*
Ruddle, H., *Strengthening Family Communication to Prevent Misuse of Alcohol and Drugs: An Evaluation Study*
Ruddle, H., Donoghue, F., and Mulvihill, R., *The Years Ahead: A Review of the Implementation of its Recommendations*
Ruddle, H., and Mulvihill, R., *Reaching Out: Charitable Giving and Volunteering in the Republic of Ireland – The 1997/98 Survey*
Ruddle, H., Prizeman, G., and Jaffro, G., *Evaluation of Local Drugs Task Force Projects*
Ruddle, H., Prizeman, G., Haslett, D., Mulvihill, R., and Kelly, E., *Meeting the Health and Social Services Information Needs of Older People*

Relationship, Relationship, Relationship

The Heart of a Mature Society

TONY HUMPHREYS
and
HELEN RUDDLE

First published in 2010 by Atrium
Atrium is an imprint of Cork University Press
Youngline Industrial Estate
Pouladuff Road
Togher
Cork
Ireland

British Library Cataloguing in Publication Data
A CIP catalogue record for this book is available from the British Library.

Paperback ISBN: 978-185594-216-5

Printed in Ireland by ColourBooks Ltd
Typeset by Cork University Press

For all Atrium books visit www.corkuniversitypress.com

NOTES ON THE TEXT
1. In the interest of protecting confidentiality, the case studies given in the book are composed
from individuals' real experiences but do not represent any one particular person's life story.
2. In the interest of a less awkward writing style, rather than using both the male and female
forms of personal pronouns we use either one or the other in alternate chapters.

Contents

Introduction

No matter where you are or what you are doing, whether you are alone or with others, you are always in relationship. Typically, we think of relationship in terms of intimate relationship between, for example, lovers or husband and wife. However, different kinds of relationships occur in all human systems and these need just as much attention as the relationship between intimates. Furthermore, each relationship is always a couple relationship, whether it is between a parent and a child, two lovers, a manager and an employee, a student and a teacher or neighbours. Any parent, teacher, politician, manager, doctor, employer or priest who sees a group as a single entity rather than a collection of individuals misses a fundamental and critical issue – each individual in that group will respond to him in a unique way. In fact, he is dealing with a number of couple relationships. If we treat all family members, employees, students, patients and audiences in the same way, we overlook the creative dynamic of the uniqueness and individuality of each human being. In reality, each child in a particular family has a different mother and a different father, each employee in a particular workplace has a different employer, each student in a particular class has a different teacher, each patient in a particular surgery has a different doctor and each client in a particular psychotherapy practice has a different psychotherapist.

There is some appreciation within psychoanalysis and psychotherapy that the therapist and the client are both individuals and that the therapeutic relationship is a unique co-creation, determined not only by the individuality of each but also by the unique story that each brings to the relationship. However, a similar appreciation does not exist widely among other professions. This book is concerned with the much-neglected area of relationships as dyads involving two unique individuals in all settings in which human beings live, work, pray and play.

The fundamental motivating factor behind all relationships is the need to belong unconditionally. If our spontaneous and real efforts to belong are not responded to then, cleverly, we find substitute ways to gain a sense of belonging. What this book will show is that there is no substitute for the real experience of unconditional belonging. It will also show how individuals try so hard to find ways to belong; but, because conditional relating never truly meets the real need for unconditional belonging, inevitably conflict emerges in any relationship where this need is not met. This book will reveal how conflict, rather than being the enemy, is the ally that attempts to attract the two individuals in the relationship back to the real quest of being unconditionally loving and loved.

This book may surprise by revealing seven unspoken secrets about our true nature and the impact of these secrets on our relationships with one another in society. These secrets have been cleverly and unconsciously devised to block the emergence of individuality and empowerment which, unless you are in a solid place of maturity, can be perceived as very threatening.

Relationships occur in the context of different holding worlds, the key holding worlds being the womb in the first instance and, later on, the family, the school, the community, the workplace, wider society and, ultimately, the self. The nature of these worlds and their impact on individuals – towards either progression or regression – are examined and, very importantly, the level of maturity required of those who head these worlds is explored. Furthermore, we outline the kinds of safe holding that are critical to the mature development of each member within these different holding worlds.

This book focuses particularly on adults' interior worlds and the interplay between these worlds and the world of relationships with others; it is especially aimed at those adults who have leadership, managerial and parental responsibilities. It offers opportunities for adults to examine closely their own inner spaces and how they relate to others in different settings – the family, the workplace, the community, corporate organisations and state institutions. We are conscious of the immense impact, for better or worse, that the architects of these social systems have on the individuals who people them. We are also conscious that many of these architects do not have safe opportunities to examine their own inner and outer lives. Unless this examination occurs, major obstruction of human potential continues and human misery is perpetuated. Whilst women tend to take a predominant role in the family, in primary and second-level education and in health and social services, men tend to dominate the corporate world, financial institutions, politics, third-level education and the sports and recreation arena. It is of serious concern that in still-male-dominated social systems, men continue to be greatly reluctant to examine their level of maturity. This book seeks to draw men into the culture of reflection and self-responsibility in relationships.

Not many professionals appear to be conscious of the fact that their individual interior worlds hugely influence their professional practice. For example, medical practitioners do not often realise that their conclusions on a patient's diagnosis and prognosis arise from the context of their own interiority. When you engage in a course of professional study, the information presented does not land on virgin inner territory but on the rich and complex, dark and light terrain of your life up to the present time. Not many of us realise that much of what determines our lives – professional and otherwise – lies at the unconscious level and will not come into consciousness until there is safety in relationships, either within the self or with others. In truth, it is astounding that individuals who hold positions of responsibility for others – parents, teachers, managers, medical practitioners, politicians, clergy and others – are not required to examine how they relate to the self and to others.

When your interior world and the world of your relationships with others go without reflection and examination, great personal and interpersonal neglect occurs. The recession that hit the financial world in recent times can be traced to deep emotional processes where trust disappeared, ethics were abandoned and people working in the financial arena had to leave their individuality, values, beliefs and reservations in a discarded briefcase outside the office door. It was not the financial institutions that played recklessly with people's money; it was not the financial institutions that were greedy and avaricious. It was individuals, particularly those at the top levels of management. It is worrying that there is still no evidence that these individuals have examined their actions and the consequences of their actions. Sadly, managers typically act as if management is a series of mechanical actions that have nothing to do with relationships and the well-being of individual employees. Among people who leave their workplace, many do so because of the demeaning treatment they have experienced from their managers. No doubt, the managers' immature, bullying behaviour is unconsciously practised, but it is an act of neglect on the part of the heads of the organisations concerned to allow such immaturity to continue.

There has generally been little consideration of psychosocial readiness for work, with perhaps the exception of the professions of psychoanalysis and psychotherapy. A means of determining psychosocial maturity needs to be developed so that individuals do not take on responsibilities they may not be even remotely ready to carry. Clearly, people who would offer such a service – relationship mentors – need to be engaged in the process of maturity for themselves. The process of self-realisation can never, of course, be totally completed but, once we have the intention to stay alert to the inevitable challenges that arise, we are in the position to be able to offer support and to model for others the process towards maturity.

Maturity has nothing to do with power, status, age, wealth, gender, profession or education, but when individuals associate their importance with such factors they become a great danger to others and, indeed, to themselves. This book will show how maturity arises from consciousness of each person's unique and individual nature, from unconditional love and from taking ownership of and responsibility for everything that arises in you – thoughts, feelings, actions, dreams, beliefs, values, aspirations, ambitions, reactions and proactions. When you possess a solid interiority – an inner stronghold that ensures that the behaviour of another cannot demean or lessen your presence in any way – you are conscious that no matter what you think, feel, say or do, it is totally and exclusively about you. Anyone who is not in that mature place will either unconsciously project onto others, blaming the world for what he feels, thinks, says and does, or introject and blame himself for what arises in him and what others do to him. The person who projects judges, criticises, bullies, dominates, controls or intimidates others, and puts labels such as selfish, lazy, useless, stupid, irresponsible, bad or worthless on the people around him. The person who introjects labels himself as, for example, useless, worthless, unlovable, stupid, bad or insane. It can be seen that there is little difference between those who project and those who introject – one is an outward movement, the other an inward one. Behind each façade lies a painful darkness. Whether a person projects or introjects, he is in no position to manage or take charge over others. Clearly the extent, frequency, intensity and persistence of these unconscious processes are major considerations. None of us, as it were, is without sin.

It may seem a truism to say that the person who has not learned to govern self cannot govern others, much less a whole country, yet the wisdom of that statement continually falls on the unconsciously deaf ears of those not ready to hear the truth. There is an urgent need consciously to create a social ethos where the pursuit of maturity is seen to be an essential – not an optional – responsibility and where the structures, personnel and supports necessary for this work are put in place. The worlds of home, classroom, school, workplace, community and society would be very different if the individuals who populated them were possessed of a high degree of maturity. This book is designed to provide the guiding framework that will enable individuals to take up the challenge of maturity in the interests of satisfying, fulfilling and effective relationships, and will enable those in social, educational and work systems to support the process of maturity.

You may have wondered about this book's title – *Relationship, Relationship, Relationship* – but there is method in the seeming madness of its repetition. If we accept that all social relationships are essentially couple relationships then, no matter what kind of coupledom is in question, there are actually three relationships that have to be examined in each. Two of these are the inner relationships with the self of each of the two individuals involved; the third relationship is the outer one between them. The critical relationship is how each partner in the couple relates to the self; it is these inner relationships that determine the outer one.

All of us manifest our interior world all the time – and not just through Freudian slips – and it is this interior world that determines the quality of our relationships with others. If we attempt to improve what happens between people without examining and resolving what happens within each of them, we cannot effectively resolve conflict in relationships. Any attempts to do so would be, in fact, a distraction from the necessary and urgent interior work being signalled by the outer conflict. This book will show how for individuals to blame each other or to blame themselves for whatever conflict arises in coupledom is a very clever – but unconscious – strategy; it postpones having to face the dark inner terrain of fearfulness, doubt, insecurity and experiences that we dare not bring to light. It is for this reason that the book will concern itself with the 'how' of personal maturity. It is the 'how' of your earlier relationships – particularly in the home – that leads to what is often a profound concealment of your true nature, uniqueness and individuality. Essentially, any person who is both troubled and troubling needs to find an unconditionally loving relationship with the self, and with at least one other, which will provide enough safety to enable the relaunching of the voyage of self-realisation, self-expression and maturity. This process calls out for great patience; the old saying, 'Once bitten, twice shy', applies here. For the many individuals who have been bitten many, many times in their early relationships, wariness in current relationships is seen at a deeply ingrained level as being necessary for survival.

This book will examine how relationships, in all their different holding worlds, can be interrupted; in particular, it sets out how emotions are responded to in interruptions, whether or not listening occurs, whether or not communication is open, direct and clear and whether or not definite boundaries are in place.

We emphasise that it is the self that differentiates each one of us from other human beings and from the rest of the universe, providing each person with a sense of 'I-ness' or 'al-one-ness', and a sense of unique presence in the world. The self is the unchanging core of us that is always wise, that knows how things are in our different holding worlds, that knows whether safety is present to be real and authentic and that devises the perfect protective strategy when we experience threat. It is the self that makes it possible for each person to give and receive love and to be responsible around ourselves and other human beings. Understanding the nature of the self is the foundation of the maturity that is essential to the well-being of human beings and the success of their relationships with others.

The central beliefs underlying this book are as follows:

- The self is the central core of everything.
- Each of us has his own individual story.
- Unconditional love is the *sine qua non* of mature relationships.
- The understanding that all human behaviour has creative

purposes and always makes sense leads to the mature resolution of conflict in relationships.

- Compassion is a key emotional response to an individual's troubling and troublesome behaviours.
- Consciousness of what lies hidden is critical to self-realisation and mature relating.
- New choices automatically arise from a raising of consciousness.
- New, authentic and real actions follow on from new choices.
- Persistent provision of support for and modelling of maturity considerably aids the process of self-realisation and mature relating.

The above beliefs are fleshed out in the following chapters, so that no stone will remain unturned in the pursuit of maturity and the freedom to realise the self. Any person who brings maturity to relationships within the social systems of marriage, family, community, the workplace, religious and spiritual community, public institutions and wider society inevitably enlightens these spheres – and, eventually, enlightens the world at large.

1. Starting Points

- The Importance of Story
- The Need to Belong
- Holding Worlds
- The Womb as Holding World
- The Family as Holding World
- The Community as Holding World
- The Wider Society as Holding World
- The Self as Holding World
- Defensive Belonging
- Substitutes for the Real Experience of Unconditional Love
- Substitute Responses Pose Threats to Others
- The Importance of Conscious Awareness
- The Self: the Creator of Real and Substitute Responses
- Identifying Real and Substitute Responses

The Importance of Story

We begin this book by emphasising the importance of recognising that all of us have our own unique stories in life and that we bring those stories to every relationship in which we are involved.

It is vital that we are sensitive to story – our own and the other's – whenever we encounter another person, either in a one-to-one interaction or as part of a group of people. Nobody can know another person's story and in relationship it is always counterproductive to make assumptions, to judge, to accuse, to diagnose, to make a prognosis or to evaluate the other person without involving her. To treat another as, for example, a 'human resource', a 'patient', a 'client', an 'employee' or an 'object of scientific study', without taking into account that person's rich and complex life-story context is to demean her presence. The experience of having her presence lessened may be the very reason she is seeking your help, or struggling emotionally, socially or physically. Unless you are sensitive to story, your response to her may be yet another nail in the coffin of her low self-esteem. Of course, story is always a two-way street; you too deserve sensitivity to your own story, both from yourself and from the others with whom you interact.

Your ability to be sensitive to the other's story very much depends on your level of sensitivity to your own story. In relationship it is very important to practise kindness – there is no greater wisdom than kindness. When you find that you are not practising kindness, then you need to reflect on your own story – again, without judgement, accusation or evaluation. If, for example, you find yourself being superior, judgemental, controlling, blaming, sarcastic, dismissive, undermining or punishing of another person's presence, ask yourself what in your own story might have brought you to this defensive position. Equally, when another responds to you in ways that demean your presence, ask yourself, 'What might have brought that person to a place where she is not able to respond to me in a way that is worthy of my dignity?' When we find ourselves unilaterally reaching for conclusions about another's actions, we are being propelled by a fear within ourselves, a fear which arises from our own life experiences. When we are in a solid mature place within ourselves we can explore with the other person what is happening in her interior world. For example, when we can ask, 'Why is it that you are being aggressive?' we are open to hearing and getting to know that person's story. There is then an opportunity for something real, dynamic, productive and mutually satisfying to emerge in this couple relationship.

It is important that we try to be sensitive to what comes out of our mouths, what our bodies may be saying and what our actions may be conveying about the extent to which we value our own dignity and self-respect, and the presence and expression of the other. You never know what you may be tapping into in another person's story. For example, a sexual vulgarity on your part in a group setting may resonate with a painful sexual violation endured by another member of the group. You will have no idea of how your expression is received by the other without knowing the humiliation and degradation she may have experienced and the impact it has had on her sexual self-expression. A further example of the need to be mindful of the potential impact on the relationship of what we convey, in another kind of setting, is the manager who derides an employee's work efforts in front of her peers without any consciousness that she is repeating a lifetime's worth of put-downs that have occurred in this employee's story. As a result, the manager seriously interrupts the relationship. We need always to be conscious in our relationships with others that very few people have escaped experiences of being ignored, demeaned or diminished in their self-expressions – physical, sexual, intellectual, emotional, behavioural, social and creative – and, as a result, everyone has vulnerabilities. The frequency, intensity and persistence of such unhappy relationship experiences are important aspects of our stories.

It is also important to be sensitive to the fact that once you interact with another human being you have become part of her story and she part of your story. Whatever is to emerge between you is always a co-creation. It is never one expert or authority doing something to another person; it is about two people coming together to explore something taking place between them, whether for a moment, an hour, a day, a month, years or a lifetime.

In our practice of exploring people's stories and, where appropriate, sharing our own, we have never ceased to be amazed at the astounding capacity of individuals to survive – although always at a cost – untold threats to their presence and their self-expression from their earliest years. No two stories are ever the same, and so our responses to each person's story need to be uniquely tailored to that story. There is no such thing as one drug for all ills, one therapy for all psychosocial problems, one way of teaching all children or one way of learning for all students.

The Need to Belong

The late poet and philosopher John O'Donohue, in his book *Anam Cara*, talks about people's deep need to belong. He says that 'people want to belong to a partner, a family, a group, a workplace'. But, in order to belong happily with others, it is crucial that I first belong with myself; if my sense of self is dependent on others then my belonging to them will always be insecure. John O'Donohue recognises this fact when he strongly advises adults to belong to themselves, not to anything outside of themselves. He describes that belonging to self as a solid interiority. If you inhabit such an interiority, nobody can demean, lessen or exile your presence in any way.

As adults, it is our responsibility to belong to self. Otherwise, any belonging to another arises from a place of emptiness and, inevitably, is dependent and controlling in nature. For example, if a manager in a workplace has little inner holding, then her insecurities and fears will be reflected in her management in behaviours such as aggression or passivity. She may be demanding, hypercritical or inconsistent. When the employees who are under the charge of that manager are not in that responsible place of belonging to the self either, then the interactions between manager and employee will create a dark relationship world, where coming to work is a threatening and painful experience rather than a joyful one. The ensuing conflict in the relationship will loudly, and urgently, call attention to the need for both manager and employee to reflect on their relationships with the self and to resolve their enmeshment with others.

Children, firstly and most importantly, need to feel that they belong to a family; later, they need to feel that they belong to relationship worlds beyond the family, such as nursery school, primary school and the local community. But whether or not a child will have a secure sense of belonging depends on the extent to which her parents, and other significant adults, have found their own belonging to the self.

The key to a secure sense of belonging is unconditional love. Going back to the work of Jung in the early twentieth century, many psychological theorists and practitioners have emphasised that unconditional love is the deepest longing of every human being, young and old (see, for example, Fairbairn, Winnicott, Lake and Sills, among others). A child who experiences the security of being loved unconditionally for herself will emerge into adulthood with a strong, conscious sense of her worth, capability and unique presence and will, therefore, belong to her self. An infant, usually, will reach out spontaneously and fearlessly for unconditional love – unless its holding in the womb world has already been unsafe – but the sad fact is that from very early in life many individuals learn to be extremely cautious and fearful in expressing their need for love and belonging. They have experienced threats – such as rejection, failure to respond, ridicule, shame and insensitivity – to their reaching out, and by staying hidden they have creatively found ways to offset those threats.

Unconditional love entails loving the child, loving the other person, for her unique and unrepeatable presence in the world. There is no room for ambiguity here – no room, for example, for expressions such as, 'I would love you if . . .' or, 'I love you when . . .'; there is no room for confusion of the person herself with her behaviour or with any particular attribute or skill – physical, intellectual, emotional, social, sexual, behavioural or creative.

Holding Worlds

In our journey through life we encounter a series of progressively wider relationship worlds – referred to in this book as 'holding worlds'. (Winnicott uses the term 'safe holding field' to refer to the extent to which the mother and others are attuned and responsive to a child's needs.) The quality of the net of relationships we experience in these holding worlds – the extent to which our presence is held with unconditional love – is a crucial influence on our well-being. The five holding worlds that are key for us in our life's journey are as follows:

- The womb as holding world
- The family as holding world
- The community as holding world
- Wider society as holding world
- The self as holding world

As adults, we may have few or no conscious memories of our experiences in the first holding worlds of the womb, early family life and early community life, even though these experiences have had a major impact on how our story has evolved. However, where there has been neglect, this will always manifest itself albeit in unconscious protective behaviours. For example, there are individuals who have no conscious memories of early gross sexual or physical violation but whose behaviours as adults (they may be asexual, sexually aggressive, terrified at the prospect of violence or violent themselves) indicate that violations did indeed occur in their life stories. It may be only within the safe embrace of an unconditionally loving therapeutic relationship that those repressed memories begin to emerge.

The Womb as Holding World

The first holding world we experience is the womb. At this stage in our journey the womb constitutes our total world. Frank Lake, based on his work on the foetus in the womb, has strongly concluded that an individual is present from the moment of conception. Accordingly, parenting needs to start at this very early stage, prior to birth. The well-being of the mother is critical to the quality of this holding world; the degree to which the mother cares for herself will impact on the well-being of the foetus. All parenting starts with self and the mother's care for herself is her most important parenting responsibility. This responsibility needs to continue when the child is born, throughout childhood and into adulthood. All the safeties a child requires for the emergence of self need to be present during the period of pregnancy. (See chapter three for a description of the safeties we need in our holding worlds.) Fathers have a responsibility to support mothers in ensuring that these safeties are present; fathers also need to take on the responsibility of being caring towards themselves.

The Family as Holding World

After the womb, the next holding world is the family. Parents and other significant caregivers are the key players in this world, although siblings also have a very important influence. In contemporary western society over forty different types of family can now be counted. Whatever the family type, there needs to be at least one adult who truly and unconditionally cares for the infant following birth. This relationship creates the security that enables the child to explore this new holding world. The continuity and quality of this adult–child relationship are fundamental to the open emergence of the child's self. If the child does not experience the necessary safeties enabling different expressions of self, she will learn not to trust the world within, and beyond, the family. The frequency, severity and endurance of the blows to her presence will determine the extent of the shadow world she will necessarily and ingeniously create.

The Community as Holding World

In the progression from infancy to childhood each person begins to encounter wider holding worlds, such as crèche, playschool and primary school. Later on, as a person enters adolescence, she encounters an expanded community that may include a second-level school, the local neighbourhood, and sporting and hobby facilities. Nowadays children can enter the holding world of community at a very young age. For example, children may be placed with child-minders within weeks of birth. Again, what counts here is the quality of the relationships the child experiences, within both the family as holding world and the community as holding world. There is no guarantee that an extended time in the family as holding world is beneficial to a child's well-being.

Since the community as holding world includes extended family, neighbours, childcare personnel, teachers, clergy and the personnel of sports clubs and other public and private amenities, the well-being of children in this holding world is the responsibility not just of parents but of all adults who encounter children and have a duty of care towards them.

The Wider Society as Holding World

Later on, as each person enters adolescence and young adulthood, she leaves behind the relative security of the family and community as holding worlds and enters the wider holding world of the society of which she is part. Many new challenges – physical, sexual, educational, professional, philosophical and spiritual – face the young person at this stage of the life journey. Among adolescents, support to take on these challenges is typically first found within the same-gender group, same-gender peers being an important influence at the beginning of the road to independence and self-reliance. Later on, the 'bosom pal' can begin to play a significant role. In mid-adolescence, sexual attraction begins to emerge. It can be quite a step to express such attraction, particularly if up to this point spending time with the opposite gender has been seen – as it often is – as letting down the group and the bosom pal. There is also a deeper issue involved: the young person needs to check how supportive individuals from the opposite gender are likely to be in her exploration of the wider world. In early adulthood, the need for a more lasting relationship with another begins to emerge. The creativity in this reaching out lies in finding a person who loves and accepts the person for her self and provides support in her various endeavours in wider society.

Of course, when a young person has not experienced safe holding in the first three worlds she will find the prospect of participating in the wider society as holding world very threatening. It is important that adults in relationship with her be alert to the inner turmoil that she may be bringing with her from her early life story.

The Self as Holding World

Being adult is about being self-reliant and independent, being able to stand on your own two feet; it is about coming into your wholeness and finding that inner stronghold of self; it is about coming home to self as holding world and operating from that solid place of interiority that John O'Donohue speaks about. The level of safety we experience in our different holding worlds – the extent to which unconditional love is present in our relationships – has a huge influence on our ability to find that solid inner place. In childhood, and to a lesser extent in adolescence, we are dependent on the adults in our holding worlds to create and maintain that safety for us but as adults we can no longer afford to remain dependent on others and must take charge of being safe in our worlds ourselves. The ultimate holding world is an inner world – the holding world of the self. This is the holding world that is always safe, always unconditionally loving. It is crucial for us that we find that ultimate holding world so that we will be able to withstand, in an open, conscious and real manner, the threats that inevitably arise in the outer holding worlds of which we are part.

Defensive Belonging

Our sense of belonging and our sense of the conditions necessary for that belonging in our early holding worlds, particularly the holding world of the family, have a major impact on how we hold ourselves in relationships later on in life. If we have had the blessing of unconditional, secure belonging then we can hold ourselves with separateness, independence and openness in our relationships. Sadly, however, not many of us have had such a blessing. As a consequence, we hold ourselves in defensive ways with others. Depending on how parents and other significant adults have responded to us, our defensive sense of belonging may be placed in one of three categories:

- Over-belonging, where the parent leads his or her life through and for the child and, thereby, creates a powerful co-dependence in the relationship.
- Under-belonging, where the parent dominates and controls the child and expects the child to live his or her life for him or her and, thereby, creates a powerful co-dependence in the relationship.
- No belonging, where the parent totally neglects the child from a place of total neglect of herself and, thereby, creates a devastating non-relationship.

It is often the case that where one parent over-belongs to the child the other parent relates in an under-belonging way. As will be seen, the child in such a situation will cleverly determine with which parent it is best to side and form a coalition against the other parent.

It has long been thought that each child is a victim of her circumstances, but our experience is that, where a lack of unconditional belonging is evident, children create their own clever and ingenious responses. Certainly, early experiences have an impact; it is also true that a child is not in a position to change the immature responses of her parents. She can, however, choose ways of being that will reduce the threats in relationship and that will gain her recognition (albeit substitute recognition) in the absence of the real response for which she longs.

Substitutes for the Real Experience of Unconditional Love

In the face of a lack of unconditional love, a child will develop a repertoire of behaviours that are cleverly designed for the following purposes:

- To offset further threats to her presence.
- To be a substitute means of getting some form of attention, albeit conditional attention.
- To alert others to the unhappy nature of the relationships being experienced – the plea being 'would some mature adult please detect the sad situation?'

The greater the threats to the need for unconditional belonging, the greater the substitute responses created.

The kinds of substitute behaviours that children creates when they experience a lack of unconditional love and a lessening of their presence may be categorised as follows:

- Acting out – attempting to counter-control through temper tantrums, refusal to eat, opposition, aggression or destructiveness. A child who acts out is often seen as a 'troublesome one' and can be labelled as 'hyperactive', 'attention seeking' and 'oppositional'. Sadly, she is often medicated for these creative responses to insecure holding.

- Acting in – attempting to gain recognition by being 'good', by being a perfectionist, excessively pleasing, hard working, dedicated, shy, timid or conformist. A child who acts in can be seen as the 'perfect child', never causing any trouble. The deep trouble within the child often goes unnoticed by the adults in her holding worlds. Children who act in are rarely labelled or medicated, but their inner turmoil requires as much attention as that of children who act out.

- Developing addictive behaviours or addictions to substances. These kinds of substitute responses are more likely where there is gross under-belonging, over-belonging or no belonging. Typical – and socially acceptable – addictions for adults are work, success, wealth, knowledge and status. The creativity of these addictions is that they bring recognition; the person can be put on a pedestal, albeit a pedestal from which she dare not fall. The more socially unacceptable addictions – to alcohol, drugs (whether prescribed or illegal), cigarettes or food – are a means for the person temporarily to fill the void within, despite the threatening complaints of others. Of course, the complaints of others constitute some kind of recognition – 'At least they see I'm alive' – but they miss the deep anguish that is present.

- Becoming ill. One of the most powerful means for children (and indeed for adults) to draw attention to their fearfulness and insecurity is to get sick. Children who are insecure in their holding worlds are masters at creating tummyaches, headaches, glandular fever, vomiting, recurring infections. By getting sick they receive the tender loving care that is not spontaneously and regularly available to them. Among teenagers and young adults, the illnesses created can be more serious and may even be life threatening. This signals that there is no more serious illness than the 'dis-ease' of not being loved unconditionally.

These different kinds of substitute behaviours are often not recognised in our holding worlds for the ingenious and wise creations they actually are. Instead, they are often responded to as 'problems', 'medical syndromes', 'bad', 'mad' or 'difficult'. Such responses only increase the level of threat being experienced by the individuals concerned and lead to existing substitute behaviours being reinforced or new substitutes being created. Unless the significant adults in children's lives resolve their own lack of belonging to self, then children will deepen and widen their substitute responses as they graduate into adolescence and adulthood. The more children progress through the different holding worlds of womb, family, community and, later on, in adolescence and adulthood, through the holding world of wider society, the more the dangers to their person increase, unless they are fortunate enough to find themselves in relationships with people who are in a mature place of self-holding. Of course, children who are fearful of showing their fullness and bring that fearfulness into adulthood become adults who, in turn, respond to the children in their lives and to other adults in over-belonging, under-belonging or no-belonging ways. This is how the sad cycle of defensive belonging is perpetuated. The cycle can only be broken when adults are provided with opportunities to become conscious of the reality of their unique presence in the world and to take on the powerful and essential task of inhabiting their own individuality.

Substitute Responses Pose Threats to Others

Any substitute response always poses a threat to the well-being of the other party in the relationship. This is clear when an individual is aggressive, violent, manipulative, controlling or abusive, but the threat to another, while equally present, is less obvious when the substitute behaviour is passive, shy, anorexic, self-harming, perfectionist, depressed or self-deprecating. The former responses are sources of threat because they show no belief in the capacity of another person to love unconditionally, and the person concerned certainly does not model self-reliance and independence. The threat in the latter kinds of substitute response resides in the individual's lack of belief in her own capacity to receive and to show straightforward love. The threat in passivity is captured in the old saying, 'When good men do nothing, evil thrives'.

No progress can occur in any couple relationship, no matter the setting, when each party to the relationship operates from a substitute place. The cycle may only be broken when one partner responds in a real and mature way. If a person responds in an unconditional way and maintains definite boundaries around her own worth and value, she will take the necessary action to safeguard the self in any interaction with the other; she will also offer the opportunity for the other person to speak and act maturely. Of course, there is no guarantee that the other individual will then feel safe enough to take up the opportunity; she may need more experience of unconditional relating before taking the perceived enormous risk of receiving, never mind giving, unconditional love. It is crucial that the person who is fortunate to be in a mature place does not give up on the other; keeping the door open to mature relating recognises that in the other person's story there may be great risk in openness. She does not want to re-experience the overwhelming quenching of the light of being that occurred in earlier life. While consciously she may have diluted the memory of the pain of rejection, at an unconscious level she knows full well its emotional devastation.

You will see, then, the utter necessity for each adult to take on the responsibility of loving and belonging to self. This is a particularly pressing responsibility for those adults who act as the heads of our different holding worlds – parents, leaders and managers in different settings such as healthcare, education, work, spiritual care and social care. Adults in these positions of responsibility need to constantly examine the state of their interior worlds and, where they find darkness, to seek help immediately (see chapter three). When those in roles of authority do not take responsibility it behoves the rest of us to challenge their untenable position in a way that, while non-threatening, is nevertheless persistent. To turn a blind eye and hope that time or some other outside force will change things would be to neglect ourselves and others in turmoil. Only the individual can effect change; the more individuals seek and speak the truth, the more stable society will become, the more productive the workplace will become and the more dynamic education will become as a psychosocial and economic power in people's lives.

The Importance of Conscious Awareness

Thanks to the work of Freud, we understand that as humans we operate at different levels of consciousness and, indeed, that most of what we think we consciously do arises from an unconscious place. For example, a manager who frequently and persistently bullies her subordinates may not be aware that her threatening behaviours spring from her inner, insecure self-holding and her fear of abandonment – which lie at the unconscious level. Any overt attempt to draw her attention to this underlying reality may very well be met with an escalation of her bullying behaviours. However, until what lies hidden comes to consciousness, no change will occur in her repertoire of substitute responses. The word 'substitute' is apt; the prefix signals the fact that the troubling response in question was formed at a below-conscious level and will remain hidden at that level until the person's holding worlds become considerably safer. There is wisdom in the unconscious formation – it keeps at bay the horror of the lack of unconditional loving experienced. It is for this reason that in individual or group psychotherapy, when unconditional love is present, an individual can release enormous pain and grief that has been bottled up in the unconscious since childhood. Over the years, individuals who have experienced this release have described it to us as a huge burden being lifted off their shoulders, producing a feeling of lightness and aliveness that they have never before experienced.

Conscious behaviour is what we know ourselves to be thinking, imagining, saying and doing; the source of conscious behaviour is very often in the unconscious. The unconscious is the realm of all the sub-stitute responses we have needed to create in order to survive 'the slings and arrows of outrageous fortune'. Consciousness of those creations will only arise when the safety of unconditional regard and non-judge-ment are present in the relationship – with self and with others. The unconscious never sleeps; it is ultimately the source of all behaviour because it is from there that the drive towards self-realisation emerges. The language of the unconscious is metaphorical and troubled behav-iour that is symptomatic of undetected inner turmoil needs to be un-derstood metaphorically, not literally. For example, a student who is constantly distracted in a classroom may metaphorically be showing how much 'off track' she feels within herself and the extent to which relationships are 'off track' at home, and possibly also within the class-room. To read the distraction literally would be likely to result in judge-ment, condemnation, impatience, criticism and possibly even a psychiatric label. Such reactive responses would serve only to exacerbate the student's distractedness, as they too would be 'off track'. Interpret-ing troubled behaviours always has to be a co-creation; unless the other party in the relationship involves the troubled person and provides enough emotional safety for that person's story to emerge, the inter-pretation will say everything about the other but nothing about the person who is in distress.

The interpretation of dreams provides an example of how to ex-plore the metaphorical nature of the unconscious. Dreams are only one of the voices of the unconscious but some dreams, particularly re-curring dreams, carry potent messages about where you are currently in your interior life and what action you need to take. A common dream is where you are driving your car at speed at night; suddenly the brakes fail and the lights fail. You find yourself hurtling into the dark-ness, terrified of crashing but unable to do anything about it. Take the dream literally and you will check the brakes and lights in your car be-fore you drive it again. Take the dream metaphorically – it has arisen from the unconscious – and you may find that you are in overdrive at work, terrified of saying no (putting the brakes on) and of failing to meet expectations, that the light has gone out of your life and you are in a dangerous darkness where you have no control of your own life. The nightmare is, as it were, a wake-up call directing you to take control of your life.

The unconscious can also speak metaphorically through the body. For example, blocked arteries can represent a blocked flow of emotions; stomach pain may signal something currently going on in a relationship or within yourself that you are not able to digest – for example, being bullied or not being able to express or act on felt anger.

The Self: the Creator of Real and Substitute Responses

An important question that arises is: who or what creates the repertoire of responses – real and substitute – displayed by each individual? Who or what operates the behaviours that come from the various levels of consciousness in the human psyche? When you consider the immense power, complexity, ingenuity, uniqueness, creativity and infinite proliferation of human responses, it becomes clear that somebody or something has to pull all the strings. The answer proposed in this book is that the creator of everything – at every level of consciousness – is the self.

Conscious of its central importance, many psychologists and psychoanalysts have attempted descriptions of the self. Some theorists think of the self as that conglomerate of psycho-emotional-social processes that gives us a sense of identity – much like Freud's concept of the ego. Others attach a meaning to self that is deeper than that which we present to the world. Jung, for example, moving beyond Freud's concept of self as ego, spoke of Self (with a capital S) as the mediator and organising principle of life, as the seat of being. Winnicott distinguishes between what he calls the 'false self', which is defensive and arises when early relationships are not unconditionally loving, and the 'true self', which is capable of mature relationship with others and arises from an unconditionally loving environment. The founder of psychosynthesis, Roberto Assagioli, describes the self as the executive function of the personality, as the co-ordinator of behaviour, as the meeting place of conscious and unconscious, as the core of our being that acts as a unifying centre, directing all the elements of our being (physical sensations, feelings, thoughts, dreams, images and so on) and attempting to bring them into a unity and a wholeness.

In this book, the term 'self' is used to mean something akin to Assagioli's definition. The self is seen here as the central core of us, which can be encapsulated as the seat of love – of giving and receiving love. Love is the essence of our nature, as is recognised in all spiritual and some philosophical traditions. Our loving potential is expressed by the self in a myriad of ways – physically, emotionally, intellectually, socially, sexually, behaviourally, creatively and spiritually. The self is not identified with any of these expressions; it is separate from them, although it is certainly the energy and wisdom behind them. The self can create, observe, direct and bear witness to these expressions of love. It knows when it is safe to engage in them and when, in our human circumstances, it is too threatening for us to express what is at our core. The self can also be seen as the only part of us that remains forever the same. It is this sameness, this undiluted wholeness which, once found and consciously experienced, acts as an inner stronghold, a solid interiority from which nobody can exile us and in which nobody can humiliate, lessen or dismiss us.

As humans, we are both vulnerable to suffering and magnificent and awesome in how we cope with and survive our painful experiences and difficult life stories, and how we sometimes even find peace and joy in the midst of them. All this applies from the first moment of existence. Even the foetus in the womb is impelled by the self, from a place of love; even the tiny toddler apprehends threats to the expression and receipt of love and wisely, if unconsciously, develops the substitute responses that enables her to withstand those threats. The awesome reality is that substitute responses encapsulate in a metaphorical way precisely those expressions of the loving self that have had to be repressed (buried at below-conscious levels) in the face of threat.

The primary project of being human is about returning to a place of unconditional love – working our way through the shadow world of substitute responses that have necessarily been created because of our dependence in the early years of our lives on parents and other significant adults who, in turn, were working through their own shadow worlds. (The responsibility for self-realisation and the path to conscious expression of our unique and loving nature are discussed in chapter nine.)

Identifying Real and Substitute Responses

It can be a valuable exercise to reflect on your current repertoire of behaviours so you may begin to become conscious of those that are of a substitute nature and those that are real. Important dimensions that need to be taken into consideration when reflecting on behaviours are their frequency, intensity, endurance in the present time and persistence over time. For example, a man may only rarely express what he feels; he may do so tentatively; the expression may endure only for 30 seconds; and this reticence may stretch back as far as his childhood. Alternatively, a woman may frequently say yes to any demand made of her; she may be intense in responding to another person's need and keen to reassure that person that it will be fulfilled – 'I'll do it, I'll do it!' That 'yes' response may stretch back for years – into her childhood, where she dared not say no, only yes, to her parents' demands.

As you examine where you are at present in your interior life, bear in mind that whatever your repertoire of behaviours happens to be, that is precisely what is required at this time in your life story. Becoming conscious of, understanding and appreciating with compassion where you are is a powerful step towards the realisation of self.

Some examples of real responses:
- Natural curiosity
- Eagerness to learn
- Love of challenge
- Emotional expression
- Emotional receptivity
- Fearlessness
- Communication that is direct and clear
- Listening without interruption
- Adventurousness
- Independence
- Spontaneity
- Living in the here and now
- Competitiveness with self, not with others
- Embracing mistakes and failures as opportunities for progress
- Acceptance of success as a step towards further progress
- Willingness to listen to feedback
- Willingness to say, 'I got it wrong'
- Separateness from others' reactions
- Readiness to apologise for unloving behaviour
- Love of work
- Enjoyment of privacy
- Ability to sit quietly in a room on your own
- Responsibility for the self and your own actions

Some examples of substitute responses
- Avoidance of challenge
- Hatred of change
- Physical withdrawal
- Emotional withdrawal
- Emotional clinging
- Fear of mistakes, failure or success

- Apathy
- Non listening
- Perfectionism
- Addiction to work, success or the approval of others
- Boastfulness
- A sense of superiority or inferiority
- Hypersensitivity to criticism
- Over-pleasing
- Rebelliousness
- Bullying
- Destructiveness
- Violence
- Verbal aggression
- Shyness
- Self-criticism
- Sulking
- Unco-operativeness
- Blaming others

When individuals – child or adult – display substitute responses such as those above, what they are exhibiting is the shadow-self screen they have necessarily and creatively constructed. Unless attention is paid to this painful reality, their well-being will remain blocked and their behaviours will pose a potential impediment to the well-being of those with whom they are in relationship.

2. Society's Seven Best-kept Secrets

- Secrets About our True Nature
- The First Secret: Each Person is a Genius
- The Second Secret: We are Creators, not Victims
- The Third Secret: What Arises in Me is About Me
- The Fourth Secret: You Always Know What is Going on in You
- The Fifth Secret: Self-reliance is Always Present
- The Sixth Secret: Each Person is an Individual
- The Seventh Secret: Unconditional Love is the *Sine Qa Non* of Conflict Resolution

Secrets About our True Nature

Society is a collection of individuals. Each individual has his own repressions; and where you get a collection of individual repressions societal secrets can emerge – things that the society dares not bring to light. Sometimes what dare not be brought to life is a darkness in our holding worlds. A recent and very troubling example of this is the secrecy there has been in our society regarding the extent of sexual abuse endured by children. Secrecy about unsafe holding is not confined to the expression of sexuality; there can be, and often is, secrecy about the existence of diminishment or degradation in emotional, intellectual and social areas of human functioning. Clearly, such secrecy has a huge impact on how we relate to one another. Here, however, we are concerned not about how darkness gets covered up but about how the light of our true nature is often obscured. We identify seven secrets in our society about our true nature as human beings. These can obstruct relationships just as seriously as the secrets about darkness:

- Each person is a genius.
- We are creators, not victims.
- What arises in me is about me.
- You always know what is going on in you.
- Self-reliance is always present.
- Each person is an individual.
- Unconditional love is the *sine qua non* of conflict resolution.

The First Secret: Each Person is a Genius

A recent book by Michael Greenberg, father of a 15-year-old girl called Sally, describes a vision the teenager had while watching two girls at the playground: she said she saw their 'limitless native little girl genius' and realised that 'we are all geniuses'. This, the daughter explained, is 'the unspoken secret we are afraid to acknowledge'. Sally saw herself as having been chosen to cure us of the suffering that all this repressed genius inflicts. Sally's own story reflects the truth that each of us is a genius in how we respond to what occurs in our lives. As a child Sally, as a result of being 'tested', had been labelled as having learning difficulties and had been assigned a special-needs teacher. At the time of her vision her parents had divorced and she had experienced a betrayal of love herself. Her father was a famous writer and intelligence was a matter of pride in the family holding world. Sadly for Sally, her vision was diagnosed as reflecting a psychiatric condition, resulting in very heavy medication with severe side effects. However, if it is interpreted in the metaphorical language of the unconscious, Sally had revealed her genius in the way she managed to capture exactly the issue that needed to be resolved for her – the lack of safety in her holding worlds regarding her intellectual expression. Sally needed her vision to be able to speak out the truth about her innate limitless intelligence and about the need for safety if that intelligence was to be openly and freely expressed.

Although Sally's secret now appears to be confirmed by science (see Shenk), the degree to which the vast majority of individuals still hide away their limitless intelligence is remarkable. To quote the writer Marianne Williamson, it seems to be that 'Our deepest fear is not that we are inadequate, but that we are powerful beyond measure.' Of course, it is clever to hide the light of your intelligence in circumstances where to assert, 'I'm a genius,' is likely to be greeted with ridicule, derisive laughter, judgement and criticism – a fate worse than death. Children become secure in their intellectual power when their genius in managing life is mirrored by the significant adults in their lives. When adults, through their own insecurity and fear of ridicule, fail to recognise their own genius, then it becomes too threatening for them to assert the genius of their children. Understandably, they fear that the children will also be subjected to ridicule. The result is that the fact of genius continues to be a secret and everyone struggles with actively believing in their power.

As with all dimensions of self-expression, intellectual security arises from unconditional love – a deep celebration and cherishing of the unique presence of the individual person that does not confuse the self with any of its expressions. If the person's self becomes confused with the expression of intelligence, then a substitute response such as addiction, avoidance or rebelliousness will arise in response to that expression. For example, teachers report that approximately 80 per cent of students aim for the average. This is a reality that makes teaching very challenging, and that has serious outcomes for society. It leads to later disengagement from work and avoidance of risk-taking and dynamic creativity and productivity. Aiming for the average is an avoidance strategy – an attempt to reduce the threat of too-high expectations on the part of others, such as parents, teachers and employers, and so to reduce the possibility of failure and rejection. The striking aspect of this strategy is its ingenuity. It manages to reduce or eliminate the greatest threat to a person's well-being – the experience of rejection in relationship.

The human being cannot be reduced to a reservoir of knowledge, to a particular skill or talent, to an examination result or to an academic degree. None of these defines us; we are immeasurably greater than anything we do, achieve, know or produce. Holding worlds, such as classrooms and workplaces, would be far more proactive and adventurous places if the unique presence of each member were cherished and if the genius each person exhibits as he lives out his life story were actively recognised. Until those who head up the key holding worlds in society can move from secrecy and shine light on their power beyond measure – even in the face of the immense dangers of rejection, ridicule and humiliation – it is unlikely that those in their charge will dare to raise their heads above the parapet of mediocrity.

The Second Secret: We are Creators, not Victims

To date, medicine, behavioural and cognitive psychology, psychiatry, psychoanalysis and educational psychology have tended to consider the person as victim. The human being is a 'victim of disease', 'conditioned by his environment', 'at the mercy of biological or chemical imbalances', 'at the beck and call of the unconscious mind', 'a victim of biological syndromes'. As a result of such a perspective, a huge industry of control therapies, drug therapies and interpretation therapies has been rolled out, particularly over the last hundred years. None of these approaches asks the individual how he views his illness, his depression, his violent behaviour or his learning difficulty. No meaning is attached to any of the physical, psychological or social symptoms that the distressed individual manifests; his symptoms are treated as a random happening with no connection to his life story. The aim is to prescribe ways of reducing or eliminating the troubling or troublesome symptoms (the exception here is psychoanalysis which, nevertheless, is prescriptive in its interpretations). The person is rarely involved in the design of the therapeutic programme, other than being convinced that he should do as he is told and take the medicine or adhere to the treatment regime prescribed. Questioning professionals is usually not encouraged and is sometimes unsafe for the client.

What often goes unappreciated is that blaming substitute responses, such as aggression, violence, depression, delusions and hallucinations, on hypothetical biological conditions such as mental illness or dismissing them as the result of conditioning or inaccessible unconscious forces does nothing to empower the individuals afflicted. On the contrary, it reinforces their status as victims and offers neither hope nor safety for the understanding and resolution of the major life difficulties being manifested. Neither does such an approach offer any reassurance or safety to those who are under threat from the substitute behaviours of the troubled person; both he and those who find him troublesome remain at risk.

Psychoanalysis understands that defensive actions are formed at an unconscious level but that discipline has not appreciated that such actions are not produced by some unconscious mechanism that somehow has a life of its own. Whether formed at an unconscious or conscious level, defensive actions are created by the self from a place of knowing. The task of the professional helper is to enable a person to bring the unresolved conflicts to consciousness so that he can actively understand and take responsibility for healing the effects of whatever traumas have been experienced – and, in turn, the effects of his reactions to those traumas on himself and on others.

The greater the abandonment an individual experiences, the more powerful the unconscious defences created. These creations are there for very necessary purposes: to reduce further experiences of painful rejection, and to alert others who are in a position to respond to the sad realities of the troubled individual's life. The troubled person always knows – even if at an unconscious level – the threats he is experiencing in his holding worlds. He knows whether or not he is safe enough in himself to withstand such threats openly, and when he is not safe he knows the exact substitute response that will encapsulate what lies hidden and needs to be brought to light when it is safe to do so.

The story of Sally, described above, provides a wonderful example of our ability to create the perfect strategies that will get us through the very painful experiences we encounter in an unsafe world.

The Third Secret: What Arises in Me is About Me

A third reality that is kept secret in society is that what arises in me is about me. Any attempt to voice this truth can be responded to with hostility. While such hostility is a revelation of the inner world of the person who is manifesting this response, it can be dangerous for the person seeking to be authentic to point this out. But, whether we like it or not, we continually reveal our interior world with every thought, word, feeling and action. When we begin the process of holding the manifestations of our interiority non-judgementally and exploring what is revealed about the relationship with the self and what new choices and actions are being called for, then progress towards maturity, self-realisation and responsibility becomes possible. Such owning and reflection will result in radically different ways of being in the world – ways that are sorely needed for the world today.

What is it that makes it so difficult to own the idea that what arises in me is about me – be it a dream, a feeling, a thought, an image, an action, a verbalisation or an illness? The answer to that question lies in the answer to another question: has my life to date been a series of safe moments with a few dangerous ones, or a series of dangerous moments with a few safe ones? If the former is the case for you, then you are more likely to be able to accept that what arises in you is about you. However, if the latter has been your experience, then owning and being responsible for what arises in you could prove highly threatening.

When I own what arises in me, I speak and act from an 'I' place, a place of responsibility and self-reliance. When I disown what arises, I tend to speak from a 'you' or 'they' place and blame others, the system, the government or perhaps God for how my life is. There is great wisdom – though not maturity – in such projections; through them I shine the spotlight of blame and responsibility onto others, thereby exonerating myself from criticism and judgement. These projections can only be resolved when a person finds enough help and support to enable him to find the inner stronghold in which no one can demean or reject him. This is the first step in being able to hold and respect everything that arises in him.

In the current global economic recession, political and financial leaders have been highly reluctant to accept responsibility for their disastrous financial, emotional and social practices; as a consequence it is highly unlikely that anything will be learned from the economic crisis. Experience has shown, time after time, that we do not learn from history. It appears that to own our mistakes, our fears, our vulnerabilities, our aggression, our greed and our rigidity is a bridge too far for many of us; but it is a bridge that each of us needs to cross. It is only when each person takes on the responsibility of understanding himself and reflecting on what goes on in his inner world that real progress can be made within society. A recurring theme of this book is the fact that it is individuals who make decisions. We cannot continue to distract attention onto institutions and systems that do not have minds or hearts. It is only by owning our individual responsibility that we can be a positive influence and bring authenticity to the people with whom we interact in the different holding worlds of which we are part.

It is not optional for us to own the fact that what arises in us is about us. It is an urgent responsibility. It is critical that, in particular, key heads of holding worlds take up the challenge of knowing the self so that they can create the emotional, social and intellectual safeties for those in their care to retain the authentic expression that is powerfully latent within them, and with which each person so eagerly starts out in life.

The Fourth Secret: You Always Know What is Going on in You

A fourth reality held secret in society is that we each understand precisely what makes us do what we do. It is the belief of many experts, including some psychoanalysts and psychotherapists, that clients lack awareness or insight into what underlies responses such as depression, anxiety, illness, delusion and violence, and that it is their job to enlighten clients on what has made them act in ways that are threatening to themselves and others. There are also many parents and teachers who feel they know what is best for children and young people and, as a consequence, provide unasked-for advice. The difficulty with such a superior position, which seems to say, 'I know what's best for you', or, 'I can understand you better than you can understand yourself', is that it shows no belief in the person's innate wisdom and creativity and his own power to safeguard his well-being. Giving advice or insight in such a way also hinders the other in examining his own interiority and finding his own answers. Furthermore, the answers provided by the expert are quite likely to be way off the mark of what is really happening within the other person, for the very good reason that the expert's answers are all about the expert and his present level of maturity. It is far more mature, and as a result far more helpful, to provide the unconditional love and safe environment that will allow the other to access his own understanding and determine his own solutions.

You may question how a person can always know what is going on within himself. You may wonder, for example, how a man who is violent towards his partner can be said to know what drives him when he appears so terribly out of control. The answer is that the understanding lies at an unconscious level. The man who is being violent creates this defensive response in order to protect himself from recurrences of early experiences of severe abandonment. The purpose of his violence is to ensure that his partner does not leave or reject him. This man's likely story is that as a child his unique presence did not spontaneously gain unconditional love and a secure sense of belonging. In the face of such abandonment, he cleverly created a substitute means of having his presence held by forcing other people to be there for him. All of these defensive responses are created by him, albeit unconsciously. At that unconscious level, he knows the pain of the abandonment experiences he has had and he knows that he has had to develop defensive strategies in order to survive what he has experienced. He has created the defence and he knows why he has had to do so. However, he has to keep that knowledge and understanding below consciousness because it would be far too painful to live every moment with the consciousness of unhealed harsh abandonment. The knowledge can only come into consciousness when he is held in the safe environment of a non-judgemental, respectful, understanding relationship.

In helping a person in distress, it is of paramount importance to keep in the mind that his substitute behaviours are meaningful in the context of his particular life story. Only he knows, in all its minute detail, what took place in the course of that story. In the helping relationship, the focus needs to be on creating the unconditionally loving environment, and the physical, emotional, intellectual and social safety, that will allow the understanding that is below the surface to rise into consciousness. Take the case of the man who, in his own words, treated his son 'like shit' and who, in the safety of the therapeutic relationship, came to understand that his harshness towards his son arose from his own harsh view of himself – 'because I see myself as nothing but a lump of shit'.

It is very powerful and liberating for a person in turmoil when he consciously realises and understands the sources of his threatening responses. With this conscious understanding comes compassion and the safety and motivation to change the nature of his relationship with himself and with others. Great patience is required in this process because, when we have been deeply hurt in our earlier lives, we are very slow to take the risk of reaching out and responding in an authentic, real and spontaneous way again. It can take years of persistent provision of unconditional love before we are willing to trust again. There is a wonderful saying, from an anonymous source, that each of us deserves to hear: 'I will wait patiently, even for an eternity, for you to become present to your precious life.'

The Fifth Secret: Self-reliance is Always Present

The fifth secret in society is that self-reliance is always present. When this fact is brought to light there can be strong reaction from others. An example of a typical comment might be, 'How can you say that somebody who lounges about the place and takes no responsibility for himself or others close to him is self-reliant?' A distinction needs to be made here between the kind of self-reliance that arises from fearfulness and that which stems from fearlessness. In the former case, self-reliance consists of defences against experienced threats to well-being; its purpose is to guard, in a substitute way, what is most precious – the self. Indeed, this kind of self-reliance will use any weapon to offset threats to well-being. When the worlds you occupy are physically, emotionally, intellectually, socially and behaviourally dangerous, powerful strategies are required to minimise or eliminate these perils and to protect what is sacred. The development of these defences is an act of self-reliance – they are all cleverly designed to reduce the possibility of emotional abandonment, harsh or violent responses, ridicule, humiliation and the lessening of your presence. Sometimes the most self-reliant thing to do is to do nothing, to avoid risk-taking at all costs or not to put your head above the parapet. This strategy says, 'If I don't do it, I can't fail; if I don't fail, I can't be rejected', and shows ingenious self-reliance. While defences do not change the threatening behaviours of others, they do reduce the impact of such behaviours. Some level of protection is put in place by keeping at a distance those individuals whose responses violate your presence and self-expressions.

Self-reliance that emerges from fearlessness – where there are few or no threats to well-being – is dynamic, productive, progressive and empowering, and safeguards well-being with strong boundaries (see chapter four). Whereas defences can lessen or demean the presence of another, boundaries affirm and support the other's presence but are also firm, definite and powerful in not yielding to the other's threatening behaviours. Complete self-reliance is rare; more usually, we are fearless in certain areas of self-expression (for example, social self-expression), whilst in other areas (for example, intellectual or emotional self-expression) we are fearful. What is important is to begin to seek out safeties, within and without, so that you can reclaim your inherent fearlessness and apply your ever-present capacity to be self-reliant to creating a fulfilling life for yourself and others, to building bridges rather than walls between people and to creating emotional, social and material prosperity for all members of society.

The Sixth Secret: Each Person is an Individual

The secrecy around the fact that each of us is a unique presence is reflected in the common complaint of the experience of anonymity – in homes, schools, workplaces, communities and churches. Anonymity is a devastating and light-quenching experience at whatever stage you may be in your life story – infant, child, teenager or adult. No one else experiences life in the way you do; no one else sees or hears the world in the way you do; no one else has the same body as you. Each person is a unique masterpiece. Because uniqueness is such a defining characteristic of human existence, it is essential that in our relationships we recognise and acknowledge the presence of individuality. Each child, each student, each employee, each patient and each client deserves to be seen in his own unique self.

As adults, it is the responsibility of each of us to inhabit our own individuality. It helps enormously when we are related to as individuals – from our earliest days – but the sad reality is that conformity and sameness are the norm. It can be perilous to assert our individuality and to uphold our right to live out our own unique existence, unless the people in our relationship worlds are secure enough in themselves not to be threatened by our difference. Difference is a major source of threat to persons without an inner stronghold. In a co-dependent relationship, the message is, 'Be like me. If you're not like me, then you're not with me'. In independent relationships, difference is highly appreciated and, indeed, can be the mainstay of them. A mature relationship is where each of the two people involved appoints the other the sentinel of his individuality. Maintaining individuality in relationship can be quite a challenge; it is not uncommon, when one of the parties begins to inhabit his individuality, for the other party – life partner, child, friend, work colleague or teacher – to react by castigating that person's bid for independence. Indeed, the other party may even violently attempt to prevent it. Such defensive reactions mirror the fact that the other does not inhabit his own individuality and the protective strategy of living life through others, rather than living his own life, that he employs.

The heads of our holding worlds have a major responsibility to occupy their own inner strongholds of individuality. When they do not inhabit their own individuality, and when they develop lean-to relationships with others, then they will demand conformity – at the cost of creativity, inventiveness, progress and dynamic development.

The Seventh Secret: Unconditional Love is the *Sine Qua Non* of Conflict Resolution

The seventh secret concerns the power of, and absolute necessity for, unconditional love in a mature society. Where there are conditions upon love in relationships there is conflict; conversely, where there is unconditional regard conflict does not need to arise. Unconditional regard is not a licence for us to do what we like. On the contrary, unconditional relating puts the responsibility for self and one's actions fairly and squarely on the shoulders of each party in the relationship. Unconditional relating is that place of 'I-ness', that place of separateness, that solid interiority where nothing is brushed under the carpet, that place where others are not held accountable for how you feel and you are not accountable for how they feel. Conditional relating, on the other hand, is a defensive means of passing the buck of responsibility for your life onto another; it is the place of 'you-ness' where communication is always about the other person. In a situation of conditional relating, consciousness that each adult is responsible for self and for everything that arises from self is absent. Conditional relating is a place of enmeshment, of entanglement, where individuals inhabit each other's space rather than occupying their own unique interiority. It is also a place of dependence, of lean-to relationships. Sadly, it is the most common way in which individuals relate to one another.

When relationships are of a conditional nature, it is because it is fearful to be separate, to be independent, to be one's own self, to reside in your own individuality, to be different, to be private and to enjoy one's own company. We know in our wisdom that conditional relating is not real relating; rather, it is an entrapment. But it can be highly dangerous in our different holding worlds to live our lives according to our own lights. In extreme cases of enmeshment, murder, violence, self-harm, attempted suicide and suicide can occur when one person attempts to step outside the conditions laid down in the relationship.

Conditions, though always protective in nature, are tyrannical. The tyranny of 'shoulds', 'musts', 'have tos', 'ought tos', 'should nots', 'must nots' and 'can'ts' can be very difficult to withstand. The holding world of the self needs to be very secure and strong in order to assert, 'I'm here to live my life and I wish you to take responsibility for your own life'.

Some examples of the more frequent prescriptions and proscriptions laid down in conditional relationships are as follows:

- 'You should be there for me.'
- 'You should take responsibility for me.'
- 'You should always agree with me.'
- 'You should be the same as me.'
- 'You should only consider my needs.'
- 'You should be successful.'
- 'You should conform to my ways.'
- 'We should do everything together.'
- 'You should let me live my life for you.'
- 'You should live your life for me.'
- 'You should not have your own friends.'
- 'You should never be late.'
- 'You must not have a different opinion from mine.'
- 'You must not leave me.'
- 'You must not fail.'
- 'You must not let me down.'
- 'You ought not to have preferences of your own.'

Conditions operate in most relationships and in all the different holding worlds in which those relationships take place. Where there is conditional relating – between husband and wife, manager and employee, parent and child, politician and citizen, teacher and student, police officer and citizen, for example – one of the parties will employ control and the other passivity to maintain the defensive status quo in the relationship. This enmeshment of defences can make it very difficult for any movement to occur. As long as conditional relating reigns, each person's progress is hugely blocked. It is incumbent on us all as adults, and especially on those who head up our holding worlds, to try to find the safety that will enable us to inhabit our own individuality. This is crucial for our own well-being and also so that in our relationships with others we allow them, too, the space to live their own unique lives. The places where we live, play, work, pray and create would be radically different if unconditional relating reigned.

3. Heads of Relationship Worlds

- Reflection: the Primary Responsibility for Heads of Holding Worlds
- Key Heads of Holding Worlds
- Key Heads in the Holding Worlds of Womb and Family
- Key Heads in the Holding World of Community
- Key Heads of the Holding World of Wider Society
- Managers as Heads of the Holding World of Work
- Leaders as Heads of Holding Worlds
- 'Seven Deadly Sins' Within the Holding World of Work
- The Creation of Safe Holding Worlds
- Key Skills for Heads of Holding Worlds

Reflection: the Primary Responsibility for Heads of Holding Worlds

Those of us in psychological practice are quite rightly required to examine, on an ongoing basis, what happens within ourselves and what happens between ourselves and those who employ our services. Every one of us has a responsibility to reflect on how we are within ourselves and how, from that place, we relate to others. For those who have any kind of governorship role in the different relationship settings in which we operate – our different holding worlds – there is a particular responsibility to continuously reflect. The extent to which these people deepen their maturity has a highly significant impact on the well-being of others and on the effectiveness of the systems or organisations involved. Although it makes sense that all adults in governing positions should be required to examine their present level of maturity and to review periodically their ongoing maturing process, no such requirement exists even for the key governors in our society, such as parents, teachers and school managers, medical practitioners, social workers, community leaders, organisational managers, public-service providers, politicians and an Garda Síochána. Ronald Reagan, in his inaugural speech, wisely asked, 'If no one among us is capable of governing himself, then who among us has the capacity to govern someone else?' An examination of how governors of holding worlds view themselves and how they interact with others needs to be seen as a very definite responsibility, not as a benign issue that they can choose to ignore.

The common tendency to equate reflection with psychotherapy, and the perception of the latter as being only for those who are 'disturbed', has been a clever way to avoid the challenge of self-reflection. There is no doubt that self-reflection is challenging and can only happen in a safe environment of non-judgement and unconditional regard. Because unconditional love is a rare phenomenon and because, as a result, adult maturity is also rare, each and every one of us is likely to have some level of 'disturbance' and some level of defensiveness that need resolution. Adults who have charge over others deserve the opportunities that will enable them to raise their level of maturity, and those over whom they have charge also deserve more mature caring and relating. Personal maturity is the *sine qua non* of effective governorship of others – governorship that comes from both the head and the heart. Certain qualities typical of maturity (described below) are required for all those adults who direct the various holding worlds that human beings live in, pass through and, very often, get stuck in. The extent to which those who head these worlds possess such qualities greatly influences the level of well-being of all within those worlds. It is vital for the well-being of society as a whole that all systems and organisations, regardless of size, provide the necessary structures and positive climate for this review process to take place on a continual basis.

Key Heads of Holding Worlds

Over the course of our life's journey we find ourselves at different times either receiving governorship from others or providing governorship ourselves. Below we consider those who have the key governorship roles in the different holding worlds of family, community and wider society.

Keys Heads in the Holding Worlds of Womb and Family

Mothers and fathers are the key governing figures in the first holding worlds of womb and family but others, such as medical practitioners, midwives, hospital nurses and community nurses, also play a critical role in supporting and, indeed, educating parents in their responsibilities towards themselves, each other and their children. Unless these supporting professions are peopled by individuals who have examined their own inner and outer practices, then what they offer professionally may not serve either the parents, their children or themselves very well. If, for example, parents express vulnerability but receive an authoritarian kind of healthcare, it is very difficult for them to withstand that response and to uphold and assert their need for a service that is more caring and considered. Care of a patient surely requires care for the patient; such an approach acknowledges the worth and dignity of all parties concerned.

When the holding world moves from the womb to the family, the parents play the central role. The maturity level of parents will largely determine the development – physical, emotional, sexual, social, intellectual, behavioural and creative – of their children's maturity. Psychologists and medical personnel rightly emphasise the importance of children reaching certain developmental milestones, but the crucial context for a child's emotional, social and intellectual development is the nature of the relationship between her and her parents.

It is not always easy or straightforward for mothers and fathers to create the necessary unconditionally loving environment for their children. Parents are likely to bring their own fears, self-doubt and vulnerability to the job of heading up this very important holding world but this is not always recognised or acknowledged as one of the challenges they face. Post-natal depression, for example, arises for a considerable number of mothers but, sadly, too often their inner turmoil is responded to with medication rather than with a loving exploration of their stories. Failure to instigate a holistic examination of a mother's depressive substitute responses may mirror a protective failure on the part of others in her holding worlds fully to examine their own stories. In such a situation, the heads of the holding worlds concerned may need more support even than the mothers themselves.

One of the great neglects in the family as holding world concerns the role of fathers – who have in general neither sought nor been offered opportunities to understand themselves or how they can be more effective as parents and as partners. It appears that mothers still do most of the parenting – in parenting courses, for example, mothers almost always predominate – so mothers too need safe opportunities to examine where they are in themselves and to notice to what degree they may have become over-identified with their parenting role. Mothers certainly need to be empowered to assert that parenting is a 50-50 responsibility with fathers. In our work with both women and men we have encountered much hidden pain arising from the experience of having fathers who were absent or, while present, physically aggressive, controlling and violent. It is a serious challenge for all adults, and particularly those who have governorship roles, to ensure that parents – the family architects – get the training and support they require to take on the multiple responsibilities of parenting themselves, so that they may also be enabled to parent their children.

Key Heads in the Holding World of Community

Compared to the situation not so long ago, children nowadays become members of the community as holding world very early, encountering adults other than their parents and medical and nursing personnel who influence their level of safety for self-expression. For example, mothers wishing to return to their own careers may be back at work within six months of birth, while their babies are put in the care of child-minders. (Contrary to popular belief, this need not be a threat to the child's well-being. The most important factor is the quality, not the specific nature, of the relationships they experience.) The saying that it takes a world to raise children perhaps applies especially to those in governing roles who have a responsibility towards children's well-being. Certainly, parents have the primary responsibility to act as sentinels for their children's well-being and to ensure that the adults to whom they hand over the care of their children do their jobs lovingly and effectively. Child-minders, childcare personnel and teachers in early learning facilities and in primary schools are the main new governors children encounter as they move out from the family as holding world. It bears repeating that these adults can have a profound effect on the well-being of the children who come into their care. Like all of us, these adults will have had

experiences in their early lives where they were not held in unconditional love and, as a consequence, will have developed their own particular substitute behaviours. Unless these individuals develop the habit
of reflection, they will bring these substitute behaviours into the holding worlds of the children in their charge. None of us consciously wants
to neglect the welfare of children; when we do become conscious of
how we may have been neglectful this needs to be embraced as an opportunity for mature progress. Burying ourselves in a quicksand of guilt
will not benefit anybody, although it has to be acknowledged that sometimes guilt is an easier pain to deal with than the deeper pain of consciousness of how we were neglected ourselves in our various holding
worlds. It may not be until other adults safely challenge us that we are
able to examine our lives.

Key Heads of the Holding World of Wider Society

New governors of a young person's destiny emerge with the move from
the holding world of family and community into wider society. The
wider society as holding world can be a scary place for a young person
to be launched into if the previous holding worlds have been of a
threatening rather than cherishing and empowering nature. Research
shows that some 20 per cent of teenagers experience undetected emotional turmoil and feel that adults will not understand what is going on
for them (National Suicide Research Foundation). Clearly, young people in the world of wider society need the safety of being in the charge
of adults who are in a mature place in themselves, but this, of course,
is not always the case. Feedback from second-level students, for example, reveals that two of their main complaints are experiences of
anonymity and disrespect from their teachers. Such complaints are a
source of concern not just for the students but also for the teachers.
Those who head up the school world – school principals, vice-princi-
pals and teachers – need to be understood as having their own vulnerabilities and defences and need to be given the support and meaningful

help that will enable them to resolve their own inner distress. Regrettably, it is still the case that teacher training does not include opportunities for the development of personal effectiveness. Many teachers – and we remember this ourselves from our early teaching careers – are fearful of exposing the very real challenges they encounter within themselves and between themselves and students and colleagues because of the very real fear of being judged not good enough. However, it is an act of maturity to ask for support and help, and an act of neglect – albeit an understandable one – not to reach out for what is needed.

In the wider society as holding world, young people encounter adults other than teachers who also have governorship responsibilities – people such as school counsellors, career-guidance counsellors, sports coaches and trainers, parents of friends, work-placement managers and, later on, managers of work organisations and teaching faculties in higher-level educational and training institutions.

Depending on the degree to which an individual has established an inner stronghold, wider society as holding world can be experienced as anything from slightly scary to absolutely terrifying. In our engagement with society we encounter many different individuals with governing responsibilities. These people are not always in a mature enough place to do their jobs effectively and efficiently and, when they are not mature, their substitute behaviours can pose a threat to us. The seriousness of this threat is exemplified by the recent revelations in western society of the hitherto unrecognised avarice, secretiveness and narcissism among the heads of important societal institutions, such as banks and other financial institutions, and among leaders in government. Economic factors alone are not sufficient to explain the worldwide recession that started in 2008; economic processes are always enmeshed with powerful, often unconscious, emotional processes. These emotional processes need to be acknowledged and resolved so that those in charge can bring mature responsibility to their governorship roles. The business models operating in our society showed themselves to be highly neglectful. Employees under extreme pressure were isolated and had their value measured solely in terms of money and productivity, and there was no scope for individuality and difference. A target-fixated mentality devoid of ethical values and trust tended to predominate. But it is crucial to see that it is not institutions nor governments that act inhumanely or unethically – it is individuals. Moreover, it is only individuals who have the mind and the heart to provide mature governorship. Responsibility always lies at the feet of individuals. The more those individuals who head up organisations resolve their immature ways, the less likely will be the re-emergence of the greed and irresponsibility that have so undermined the economic well-being of western society. It is crucial that the selection procedures of work organisations ensure that those who hold positions of governorship are provided with opportunities to examine how they are within themselves and how they relate to others.

Managers as Heads of the Holding World of Work

In one way or another, managing is one of the world's most common jobs – whether in families, schools, workplaces, public bodies or government – and yet it appears that mediocre management is the norm. Distressingly, research has shown that people who leave their jobs do so most often because of stressful experiences with managers. Financial institutions and, ironically, caring professions have been identified as the two sectors where bullying is most common. It needs to be recognised that the demands placed on managers can often be virtually impossible to meet; they are expected to have very wide-ranging skills in areas as diverse as finance, cost control, resource allocation, product development, marketing, manufacturing and technology. There are also demands on managers to be able to employ strategies such as persuasion, negotiation and problem-solving, and to have writing and public-speaking skills.

Perhaps reflective of these kinds of pressures, a study led by

O'Boyle and Corscadden found that many managers perceived their quality of life to be low, as they themselves judged this on the Schedule for Evaluation of Individual Quality of Life (SEIQoL), using their own frame of reference of the things they considered most important in terms of quality of life. When compared with a group of patients with a variety of conditions, it was found that on average newly appointed managers using their own frame of reference rated their quality of life at a lower level than did patients with peptic ulcer disease who similarly used their own frame of reference. Among a small group of senior managers, it was found that, on average, using their own frame of reference, they rated their quality of life at a lower level than did any patient group. While these findings do not mean that the quality of life of managers is objectively lower than that of people suffering illness, the findings do suggest that some managers may need to change their frame of reference in regard to what makes for quality of life.

In many ways, management can be seen essentially as a practical effort to get things done and to ensure that many people operate efficiently at different levels of status and responsibility. This is a role that clearly requires qualities such as persistence, endurance, hard work, concrete intelligence and analytical ability. But management of others is not just about practical strategies, techniques and qualities. The most important requirement of a manager is to ensure that the interactions within her organisation are of a nature that enhances relationship and promotes well-being. A central task of the manager is to be able to get beneath her own and others' defensive reactions to what lies hidden. While seeking to understand defensive behaviours, the manager must not dilute their impact on herself and on others. On the contrary, it is only by being able to call a spade a spade that real progress can be made. In being direct and open, however, the manager needs to be non-judgemental and empathic. When this is not the case, then understanding becomes threatening rather than enlightening in nature.

Regrettably, the training of managers does not often recognise that they are responsible for creating the environment that supports the process of maturity, both within themselves and for others in the organisation. Managers deserve the kind of training that provides opportunities for them to understand the processes that take place in our inner worlds so that they can better understand and respond maturely to any challenging behaviours exhibited by those over whom they have charge. Mature management is only possible when individual managers possess a high level of personal maturity.

Leaders as Heads of Holding Worlds

Leadership is different from management but leadership is not somehow more valuable than management, as is often thought; nor is it a replacement for management. These are two distinct and complementary modes of action. Leaders and managers operate in very different ways, mirroring their interior worlds and the different ways in which they managed to get recognition as children. Leaders are fuelled by being different, by being creative and by being innovators. Leaders may work in organisations but they never belong to them. Their self-esteem does not depend on work, on membership of particular social systems, on work role or on social status. However, leaders can be restless individuals and have the potential to create chaos in an organisation unless mature management is present. Furthermore, if a leader confuses her sense of self with her creativity and inventiveness, she can be vulnerable to any perceived criticism or rejection of her ideas.

Leadership is critical to continued progress in the wider society as holding world, yet the development of managers takes precedence over the development of leaders. The development of leadership starts at a very early age. All children in a family create their own particular responses to the family dynamic. The child who becomes a risk-taker and a non-conformist, if encouraged towards personal mastery, may well become an adult who initiates change in an organisation and who can give direction in coping with change.

'Seven Deadly Sins' Within the Holding World of Work

When we come to participate in wider society, work, whatever its nature, plays a very important part in our lives. In Kahlil Gibran's view, 'Work is love made visible', but, sadly, the loving potential of work is rarely realised. In a variation of Gandhi's 'seven deadly sins' of modern society, we have identified 'seven deadly sins' that undermine safety in the holding world of work:

- Organisations without humanity.
- Leadership without maturity.
- Management without relationship.
- Work without dignity.
- Ethos without mature ethical practice.
- Profit before people.
- Success without separateness.

Of course, it is not organisations but individuals who engage in these dark processes. Those individuals who lead, manage and head up workplaces have a particular responsibility in this regard, because it is they who largely determine the workplace culture.

Human-resources departments that relate to employees as a resource rather than as distinct and sacred individuals are an example of organisations without humanity. Other examples are employers who treat employees as cogs in a wheel or who exploit their labour. As already described, leaders, managers and heads who are not in a mature place within themselves can engage in behaviours that darken the presence of those in their charge. Those in command always need to ensure that the work they ask of employees is worthy of their dignity. The employees themselves also need to make this assessment; when work is not as they deserve, then they have serious questions to ask regarding their continued participation in that work.

In the years leading up to the 2008 world economic recession there was an unravelling of trust in respected market participants; such trust is the foundation of any strong and efficient financial system. Behaving ethically involves seeing beyond ourselves so that others in relationship with us – for example, shareholders, customers or employees – can be confident that we have their goodwill in mind and in heart. It will take considerable time to rebuild the ethos of trust that has been lost. Setting ethical guidelines will not be enough for this; only a focus on personal maturity will make this happen.

Two of the contributing factors to the crash of capitalism have been depersonalising employees and putting profit before people. Leaning on achievements, wealth, profit or success creates profound levels of insecurity that, inevitably, destabilise social and economic prosperity. The creation of wealth and profit needs to take into consideration the emotional and social processes that uphold the dignity of employees and customers, and enhance relationships between all the members of the organisation involved.

The final 'deadly sin' – success without separateness – refers to situations where a person's sense of worth is enmeshed with her success in whatever her field of endeavour happens to be. Success addiction, particularly among men, is a common phenomenon, leading to great pressure and strain not only on the person who is addicted but on all those working closely with him. One of the reasons why, in times of recession, suicide figures rise is that failure terrifies those addicted to success. Death presents itself as a less painful option than living with the anticipated abandonment that follows failure. What counts within workplaces is progress, and progress depends on the learning that arises from the natural and creative rotation of failure and success. Fixation on success and fear of failure have become huge obstructions, not just to economic progress but also to emotional, intellectual, behavioural and creative progress.

The Creation of Safe Holding Worlds

A particular responsibility lies on the shoulders of those with governing roles in our different holding worlds to create the safeties that will enable and support all persons within each particular world to come into and inhabit their own individuality. The responsibility of parents and teachers in this regard may be more readily accepted than that of managers and leaders in wider society. Nevertheless, the creation of safety is a responsibility for anyone who has charge over others, regardless of the particular holding world. This is a challenge that can prove difficult, since each person can only give from where she is within herself. If the challenge is not taken up by heads, their immature practices must be confronted so that threats are not perpetuated in our holding worlds.

The creation of an overall safe holding world involves taking into account what individuals need in order to be able to be open and real in each different form of self-expression available to us – physical, emotional, social, intellectual, behavioural, sexual and creative.

Some of the fundamentals in the creation of safety regarding our different self-expressions, in any given holding world, are as follows:

PHYSICAL
- A physical environment that is worthy of each member's dignity and ensures bodily well-being.
- Acceptance and appreciation of and respect for each individual's unique physical appearance – this means no derisive comments on size, shape, looks or height, and no comparisons with others.
- Acceptance of and responsiveness to the information and wisdom we carry in our bodies.

EMOTIONAL
- The expression of unconditional regard for each individual in

the system.

- Support and encouragement for members to be both emotionally expressive and receptive, and to use the vital information on well-being that their emotions provide.
- Recognition of the destructive power of words and sensitivity to the emotional impact of one's communication.

SOCIAL

- A culture where the presence of each person is unconditionally valued.
- Provision of firm, but non-judgemental, challenge when the behaviours of any member threaten the well-being of other members, and the support of all members to uphold their own dignity.
- A culture where individual members know that their presence in the system makes a difference and that they are missed when they are absent.
- Encouragement of and support for communication between members that is direct and clear, and support for genuine and respectful listening.

INTELLECTUAL

- Support and encouragement for each member to live life according to her own lights.
- Affirmation of our limitless intellectual capacity as human beings.
- Avoidance of labels such as 'slow' or 'bright'.
- Avoidance of comparisons and expressions of superiority.
- Acknowledgement of the difference between knowledge and intelligence.
- Realistic expectations.
- Provision of opportunities to explore intellectual potential.

BEHAVIOURAL

- A culture where it is understood that all behaviours are meaningful and where there are active attempts to uncover the meaning behind challenging behaviours when they are exhibited.
- Avoidance of labels such as 'positive' and 'negative', 'adaptive' and 'maladaptive'.
- Acknowledgement of the difference between the individual and her behaviour.
- A culture where each person is valued for her presence and not for her achievements and attainments, and where the effort and not the person is praised.
- Avoidance of judgement, comparisons, sarcasm and cynicism.

SEXUAL

- Celebration of sexuality as an integral aspect of human nature.
- A culture that recognises that each person's sexuality is for her, and is for her to decide how she wants to express it.
- Avoidance of representations of sexuality, through whatever medium, that demean, exploit or endanger others.
- The creation of firm boundaries that protect each individual's sexual integrity.

CREATIVE

- Encouragement for individuals to express their difference and uniqueness.
- Acknowledgement that each one of us is a creator in that we are always finding exactly the right ways of responding to the particular circumstances that occur in our unique life stories.
- Acknowledgement of the difference between our innate creativity and our outward inventions or products.
- Recognition of the fact that failure is an integral aspect of the creative process.

Supporting individuals in their various self-expressions does not mean giving them a licence to do what they like – a licence some children are given by parents who confuse spoiling with loving. Freedom to express carries the responsibility to do so in a way that does not threaten or jeopardise the rights and well-being of others. When expressions are threatening in nature, they need to be firmly challenged so that safety between the people concerned is restored.

Key Skills for Heads of Holding Worlds

Whatever holding world you may head up – family, school, community, workplace or part of the wider society – there are certain skills that are key to creating a safe, effective, productive and empowering environment. Many of these skills have been highlighted already in previous sections of this chapter; here we provide a summary of what is needed. As head of a holding world you need to be able to do the following:

- To reflect continuously on your own interior world.
- To be able to hold the self and be authentically self-reliant.
- To be able to understand – get underneath – substitute behaviours in yourself and in others.
- To enable others to uphold their own dignity and self-respect.
- To enhance relationships with and among all members of the particular system involved.
- To create a safe and dynamic ethos.
- To motivate and secure members' co-operation.
- To challenge whatever dark processes may be operating within the system.
- To understand the fundamental human processes in which all individuals engage.
- To resolve conflict when it arises.
- To engage in direct and clear communication.

- To listen actively.
- To stay separate from the responses of other members of the system.
- To respond to failure and success as opportunities for further progress.
- To maintain definite and clear boundaries around the position of head.
- To confront the substitute behaviours of members of the system that threaten the well-being of others and the goals of the system.

You may think it a tall order to be expected to have or to develop such skills but when we choose to take on a governing role we need to prepare ourselves for the major responsibilities that accompany that position. Knowledge and skill in your particular area of activity – parenting, education, business, finance, science, medicine, public service, politics and so on – are necessary but they are not even remotely sufficient when it comes to governorship of people. The assumption has been that if you have a qualification or training in a particular area of expertise, that is adequate for the move to a governorship role. Governing others is a profession in itself and requires a depth of training and preparation equivalent to that required for other professions.

The most fundamental obligation is to know our own unique nature and to harness the amazing potential of the self to enhance our own well-being, that of others and that of our organisation. The exploration of our own inner world is the *sine qua non* of effective governorship. When we operate from a place of emptiness, doubt, insecurity, fearfulness or vulnerability, our behaviour towards others will mirror that dark interiority. When we do not examine our internal and external lives we can create a trail of havoc. Once we adopt responsibility for the self and our actions and begin to recognise the creativity we exhibit in living our lives, then living becomes a much more dynamic and progressive experience.

4. The Importance of Boundaries in Relationships

- Where does the Conflict Originate?
- The Difference Between Boundaries and Defences
- Common Boundaries and Defences
- Differences Between Adult-Adult and Adult-Child Boundaries
- Actions Speak Louder than Words

Where does the Conflict Originate?

When conflict arises in a relationship the most common response of the two people involved is defensiveness, with the inevitable result that the conflict escalates. But there is creative purpose to conflict – it provides the opportunity for the two individuals in conflict to examine their own interior worlds and to look at the insecurities and fears they are bringing to the relationship. While conflict signals the need for reflection, examination of the inner relationship with the self can be very challenging. Recourse to a counter-attack (attack being the best form of defence) or to physical or emotional withdrawal can often seem the safest reaction. In our wisdom, we will stay in a defensive place until we have sufficient safety, both within ourselves and in our outside holding worlds, to be authentic and real. As we have seen, our defences are not designed to hurt another but rather to prevent the recurrence of painful experiences of rejection and hurt. While our defences are wise and purposeful, it is important for our relationships that we find ways of responding maturely when the distress flag of conflict is raised.

The critical issue in conflict with another is not, 'How can I live with you?' but 'How can I live with myself?' Conflict arises from what each individual brings to the relationship in terms of his own interiority. It is the meeting between the interior worlds of individuals that gives rise to conflict, not the relationship between them. As long as each person defensively believes that the relationship is the problem, little or no change will occur. Furthermore, it is only change within individuals that effects enduring change between them.

The Difference Between Boundaries and Defences

It is only possible to resolve conflict in relationships when individuals create boundaries rather than defences. A boundary calls for an action for the self, whereas a defence leads to an action against either another or yourself. A boundary is a line you draw around your own worth and dignity as a unique human being; it marks that stronghold of self in the face of threats to your well-being and it enables you to hold an inner solidity in which nobody has the power to lessen your presence. Setting boundaries is a proactive rather than a reactive process, which involves confidently taking responsibility for the self and for your own actions. Setting boundaries is an active assertiveness of your own, and the other person's, worth, value, dignity, individuality and sacredness. When conflict arises, a person who is in a fearless, self-reliant place will resort to boundaries and take definite action for the self; he will do so in a way that does not threaten the well-being of another.

This is more easily said than done, as it is only through continual reflection on our inner world that such maturity becomes possible. An expression of a boundary created in answer to somebody trying to force a particular response to a need would be, 'I'm taking in what you are asking of me but I need to be taken into account in this too. It does not feel right for me to do as you're asking.' This response means that you hold your dignity, you are open to looking at other options and you have provided the other person with the opportunity to examine his own defensive attempts at control in the relationship. Of course, there is no guarantee that the other person will take up that opportunity; but as long as one person stays in a solid place of boundary the conflict will not escalate and responsibility will be left with the person who remains defensive to examine his own reactions. The person who is being proactive in the relationship is already in that place of self-responsibility.

Common Boundaries and Defences

There is an infinite number of ways of being defensive and a corresponding richness of language to describe defensive responses. By contrast, when it comes to describing boundaries, the language available is poorer. Indeed, most people have difficulty in providing even a few examples of boundaries. This difference is not surprising, as lean-to, dependent relationships – which are moulded by the defensive responses of each party – are far more common that lean-on-yourself, independent relationships – which are created by the existence and practice of strong boundaries on the part of both parties. In a co-independent relationship each appoints the other the guardian of his wholeness – 'I trust you to safeguard your own well-being and you trust me to safeguard my well-being'. In a co-dependent relationship, on the other hand, there is enmeshment of responsibilities – 'You look after my well-being and I'll look after yours' – which inevitably leads to conflict. Each person's well-being is something only he can look after effectively. Independent relationships are always marked by separateness. Each party stands apart from the other and, paradoxically, offers the deepest and most enlightened closeness.

In troubled relationships defensiveness tends to be a two-way street. More often than not the two individuals employ defences that are opposite in nature. For example, one acts out and the other acts in – different defences but each equally powerfully protective. In mature relationships, boundaries are also a two-way street and, though these may be expressed in different ways by each member of the couple, the same fundamental message is delivered by each person: 'I am responsible for my own well-being and I will not compromise my boundary position. This is as much an act of love for you as it is for myself.'

The more common patterns of opposing defensive responses found in couple relationships are as follows:

- Aggression/passivity.
- Manipulation/compliance.
- Possessiveness/elusiveness.
- Bullying/timidity.
- Blaming/hypersensitivity.
- Criticism/obsequiousness.
- Rigidity/apathy.
- Threatening/recoiling.
- Hostile humour/collusion.

- Passing the buck/taking the buck.
- Domination/submissiveness.
- Control/submission.
- Loudness/shyness.

It can be seen that in these patterns of opposing defensive responses each bilaterally reinforces the other and the relationship becomes locked into a defensive cycle. The only hope for change is when one of the two parties responds with a boundary and holds steadfastly to it. Such a mature response mirrors an inner shift – a consciousness of the need to uphold his dignity and integrity. Of course, there is no guarantee that the other person will respond in kind but that must not deter him from maintaining and strengthening the interior changes he has made. He will do himself and the other person no favours by returning resignedly to the defensive status quo.

However, in highly threatening situations (where, for example, there may be danger of violence) a conscious decision to return for the time being to existing defences may be required until some safe refuge has been established.

Outlined below are some of the more common examples of uncommon boundaries that those adults who are determined firstly to belong to themselves aspire to, so that they bring a mature responsibility to whatever relationships they have in their lives:

- Creatively seeking out time on their own.
- Saying no to what is not right for them or what compromises their dignity, integrity or self-respect.
- Saying yes to what is good for them and affirms their dignity, integrity and self-respect.
- Setting clear and definite limits in regard to what behaviour is acceptable to them and what is not acceptable.
- Being authentic in the expression of their beliefs, values

and needs.

- Being genuine in their responses to and actions towards others.
- Being spontaneous in the expression of feelings and ideas.
- Setting a definite limit to any uninvited intrusion into their lives.
- Putting a definite stop to any attempt to impose on them artificial goals and aspirations.
- Being a strong advocate of the dignity and human rights of others.
- Not standing by when others are under threat.
- Communicating directly and clearly and speaking for themselves.
- Following through on action they have asserted an intention to take.
- Speaking and acting from the 'I' position.
- Being willing to employ backup social and legal supports to maintain boundaries.
- Owning and taking responsibility for their words, actions and inaction.
- Owning a responsibility to but not for the well-being of another.
- Speaking their own truth.

You can see that boundaries mirror an inner stronghold, and fearlessness, while on the other hand defences mirror an inner turmoil and deep fearfulness. It is also clear that boundaries arise from unconditional love and are also an expression of that love.

When you consider how the above examples of defences and boundaries may apply in your own life, it is likely that you will find that with particular individuals and in particular situations you operate from a place of boundaries, whilst with other individuals and in other situations you find yourself resorting to defences. This is very common. For example, with a good friend you may find yourself being real and authentic whereas, for example, in a discussion of deadlines and profits with your boss you may find yourself in a defensive place, feeling small, frightened, unsure and wishing the meeting would end. Alternatively, you may find that you feel very solid in yourself in the work environment but feel like a chastened child in your relationship with your mother.

The 'W' Questions

Willingness to notice is the first step towards becoming conscious of your defensive responses which, as you will recall, operate primarily at an unconscious level. There is a set of 'w' questions that are helpful in the noticing process: the 'who', the 'what', the 'where', the 'when' and, most importantly, the 'why' of your responses. It is useful to assess your responses to the 'w' questions along the continuum of least threatening to most threatening. The least threatening 'who' may be, for example, a work colleague and the most threatening may be your father. The least threatening 'what' may be discussing plans for the future and the most threatening may be the topic of how unhappy you are in your marriage. The least threatening 'where' may be out for a night with some friends and the most threatening may be a performance appraisal at work. The least threatening 'when' may be the time when you are at home with your partner and the most threatening may be when your mother-in-law visits. The least threatening 'why' – which is always an inner issue – may be a fear of letting others down while the most threatening may be a fear of being let down by others.

Differences Between Adult–Adult and Adult–Child Boundaries

The creation, nature and maintenance of adult–adult boundaries is different from the creation, nature and maintenance of boundaries between adults and children or teenagers. In adult–adult boundaries each individual operates totally from his own interiority and does not invade the interiority of the other. If he does he has stepped out of boundary and into defence. For example, if you make an 'I' statement – 'I'd like some quiet time for myself' – that is a boundary. If you follow it up with, 'and don't you disturb me', you have crossed the line into defence, because you are now putting responsibility for your need for privacy on the other person. You would have stayed inside your boundary if you had added, 'and I would like not to be disturbed'. If you are being defensive, you will either be in the other person's space ('You should have called me') or allowing him to invade your space ('If that's what you want me to do').

Defences are either an attempt to make another responsible for your well-being or an attempt to take responsibility for everybody else's needs except your own. Boundaries in adult relationships make a very clear statement regarding responsibility: 'I am responsible for myself and for my actions and you are responsible for yourself and your actions.' Adult–adult boundaries also incorporate a responsibility to the other in the relationship. You wish to interact with the other in a way that is worthy of his dignity. This automatically arises when you have a sense of your own dignity. It is in this sense that dignifying yourself is not a different issue from dignifying another; the former gives rise to the latter.

When it comes to adult–child relationships, boundaries operate somewhat differently. (The issues involved in these relationships are discussed fully in previous books: *Self-Esteem: The Key to Your Child's Future* and *Leaving the Nest: What Families Are All About*). The key difference is that in these relationships adults have responsibility for children aged up to eighteen; accordingly, it us up to the adults to establish strong boundaries around their responsibilities. Children, especially teenagers, may struggle with this. It is important, then, that from infancy, when dependence is virtually total, the adults involved set their boundaries in a consistent and committed manner. One of the main tasks of parenting, and of teaching, is gradually and in an age-appropriate manner to provide opportunities for children to take responsibility for themselves – a transition that is not generally well charted for young people by the adults in their holding worlds. Effectively, at the age of eighteen, parents and teachers need to have stepped back totally from the young person's space. If this retreat has been done step by step over the years, the transition for the young person, and for the adults involved, should be relatively easy.

Actions Speak Louder than Words

We emphasise again that defences are not mad, bad or sad; rather, they provide some kind of comfort zone until a shift of consciousness enables movement towards unveiling the truth of your unique person. The greater the defences of others in relationship with you, the greater the comfort zones that need to be created. Coming out from behind defensive walls is necessarily done in tentative baby steps because the 'enemy' – other people's defensive responses – is still out there.

The creation of boundaries needs to be done with caution but also with determination. Support from others who operate from a place of boundaries helps enormously but nobody can do it for you. The development of a loving relationship with the self – which can be undertaken in unobtrusive ways for a period of time so that others will not be threatened too early on in the process – leads to the beginning of a stronghold within yourself. At some point your quest for independence will be spotted by significant others in your life, who may still be in defensive, co-dependent places. These others may verbally rubbish anything you say or anything you may be reading about self-reliance, independence and living your own life. Sometimes the best response is no response; rather, you should quietly continue your own quest for maturity. After all, their behaviour reveals their fearfulness and that is something you cannot do anything about; that matter needs to be left in their hands. It would be a defensive action to attempt to argue your point – it is not others you need to convince, only yourself. Certainly, you can make a clear statement: 'This is something I need to do for myself and I would value your support.' Say it once and then leave it. If, however, the verbal taunts were then to escalate or there were threats of physical violence, actions would be required to safeguard the self. This may mean breaking your silence on the untenable situation to others who could provide mature support. You may wish to report incidents to your medical practitioner or contact a solicitor, a refuge centre or the police. It is important to estimate the level of risk to you when you take such actions but to persist and find a way to continue without jeopardising your well-being.

Defences in relationships are not always so terrifying and following through with assertive action can give rise to some milder reactions – such as disagreement, emotional withdrawal, sulking, hostile silences, physical withdrawal or blaming your psychotherapist or new friendships you may have developed for the changes you have initiated. Whatever the nature of these defences, if you stick to your guns and remain non-threatening, more often than not your developing independence will show benefits in the relationship. It will also provide opportunity for the other's movement towards maturity.

5. Emotions Call for Motion in Relationships

- Feelings are Taboo
- Emotions are Our Allies
- The Power of Anger
- The Power of Depression
- Are Men Heartless and Women Loving?
- Is a Good Row Good for You?
- Professional Affectiveness

Feelings are Taboo

It seems that there are over 650 words in the English language to describe different feelings. The most commonly used are 'love', 'joy', 'fear', 'anger' and 'sadness'. When we experience love or joy we are in a state of welfare, and when we experience fear, anger and sadness we are in a state of emergency. Feelings arise spontaneously and creatively in response to what is happening within and without our worlds. For example, when I inwardly affirm my own individuality I feel power but when I imagine myself making a fool of myself at a forthcoming interview I feel fear. Similarly, when I encounter somebody who appreciates the help I have provided I can feel joy but when I meet somebody who is aggressively critical I may feel anger or, again, fear. Feelings then alert us to what is going on inside and outside us at any given moment. Emotions are the most accurate barometer of the level of our well-being and, as such, need to be embraced as our allies.

There are two dimensions to emotional maturity: emotional expressiveness and emotional receptivity. Emotional expressiveness is about revealing and responding to your own feelings as they arise in you, with the realisation that they are about you, the person experiencing them. On the other hand, emotional receptivity is about being open to another's emotional expression and holding to the realisation that what is being expressed is not about you but is about the person who is experiencing the feeling, whether it is one of welfare or emergency.

It is easy to appreciate the supportive nature of welfare feelings (such as love, joy, contentment and security) but emergency feelings (such as fear, anger, depression and guilt) are often perceived as enemies rather than allies. Many individuals are very fearful of emergency feelings – both of expressing them and of responding to them in another; indeed, fear of welfare feelings is also not uncommon.

An important question for us to ask is: how did something that is such an integral and essentially wise part of our nature come to be so strongly obstructed in our society? Encouragement to be receptive and expressive of our different emotions is a relatively recent phenomenon. Many of our holding worlds still do not value – and often punish – the perception and expression of emotions. In many workplaces, for example, a taboo on feelings exists, as it does in many schools. Within families also there can be a ban on emotional expression. This is perhaps more the case for male children than female children, although girls too can suffer from a ban on feelings perceived as negative, such as anger, resentment or jealousy. Children frequently get such messages as, 'You can't feel like that', 'There's no need to be angry', 'Don't be so intense', 'Don't let them see your fear – they'll take advantage of it', 'You need to keep your feelings under control', 'Stop being such a coward', or 'I'm proud you put on such a brave face'. But feelings do not disappear because we are told not to have them. Feelings spontaneously arise; they are there to alert us to our needs or to the reality of unmet needs. When individuals repress or suppress their feelings in a creative and protective response to the dangers of emotional expression, those feelings find substitute means of expression – for example, in substance addictions, in illnesses or in emotional outbursts that seem to come out of the blue.

Perhaps one of the reasons why feelings are often still taboo is the fact that feelings never lie. When facing and speaking the truth carry many dangers, we cleverly shoot the messenger – our emotions. You have seen in chapter three that several safeties need to be consistently and predictably present for people to speak their truth – to be open, spontaneous and real in their relationships with others. When these safeties are not present – when it is highly threatening to reveal reality – is it any wonder that we repress, bottle up, displace, project, introject, modify, dilute or deny our emotions?

In terms of the well-being of children, and their roles as future members and heads of social systems, it is critical that the adults responsible for their care and education do not continue the taboo – that they allow them to express their honest feelings and communicate to them that they are pleased to hear about those feelings. The most powerful way for children to be supported and encouraged to be emotionally in tune with themselves is for the adults around them to model emotional authenticity. This means expressing openly how they are feeling, in a way that shows that they own and take responsibility for these feelings and for whatever actions might need to be taken in response. Children necessarily take their cues from adults, so it is crucial that all the significant adults in children's lives model emotional expressiveness and receptivity.

Emotions are Our Allies

Emotions arise spontaneously and accurately mirror our interior world at any particular moment; this is why they are such important allies for us in living our lives. The distinction between emergency and welfare feelings is important, as they signal different inner states. But despite the fact that emergency feelings are often perceived as negative, they are also our allies in supporting our well-being. Welfare feelings – such as joy, peace and excitement – arise to let us know that our well-being is being safeguarded, while emergency feelings – such as anger, fear, sadness, guilt, jealousy and disgust – can alert to a relationship emergency and to the need for action in the face of some threat to well-being. If we have a secure inner stronghold then we can respond to our feelings in an open, direct and real manner. When this is not the case, our responses will necessarily be defensive in nature. Even when we respond defensively to our feelings – for example, when we respond with aggression to a feeling of anger – the feeling itself is always right.

Emergency feelings emerge in response to perceived threats to our well-being. The word 'perceived' here implies that what determines each person's response to a threat – emotional, sexual, physical, intellectual or social – is the level of security felt within. Two people's emotional responses to the same threat – for example, to the same criticism, or to their manager's bullying – can be totally different. In the workplace example, each employee's unique response is a function of her level of emotional security, and the manager's bullying, whilst always threatening to the well-being of others, is not the direct cause of a particular employee's response. Of course, it is crucial that the manager examines what it is within her that is giving rise to her bullying, and that she take responsibility for whatever unmet needs she may be experiencing. It is equally crucial, however, for the employees to examine their own emotional reactions – particularly those who feel most distressed – so that they can be more empowered to withstand the manager's threatening behaviour. The most important question for the employee to ask is, 'What do I feel when the manager behaves in a bullying manner?' Similarly, the manager needs to ask the question, 'What am I feeling when I start bullying?'

Emergency feelings are our most reliable guide to the threats that are present and to the need to find inner safe holding so that we can withstand the defensive behaviours of others. When the person at the receiving end of threatening behaviour is quite solid and secure, emergency feelings will prompt an assertive safeguarding action to reduce or eliminate the threat. For example, if this person's boss harangues her in front of her colleagues, she will respond to her feelings of anger or fear or distress or humiliation quite definitely: 'John, two things. One, when you need to talk to me about an issue that is bothering you, please do so in private. And two, talk about your unmet needs rather than being verbally aggressive with me.'

Such a mature response is rare; the more common responses are to attack back, to swallow down the emergency feeling and passively take the tirade, or to get up and remove yourself from the scene without explanation. When you passively remove yourself from the scene, you are showing, albeit unconsciously, how you are removed from respect and care for yourself. Equally, when you attack back – or perhaps later gossip maliciously about your boss – you are in a disconnected place within yourself. Whatever your defensive response, you need to urgently find the support to reclaim your care of self so that you no longer tolerate the threatening responses of others. In erecting boundaries around your dignity, it is important that you yourself do not become a source of threat to others.

When you are operating from an inner place of fearfulness, the kinds of defensive responses to emergency feelings you are likely to show include the following:

- Blaming yourself – 'I'm so pathetic.'
- Blaming another – 'You make me so angry.'
- Diluting – 'It's not so bad really.'
- Neutralising – 'What I'm feeling is the same as anyone would feel.'
- Displacing – 'This house is driving me crazy,' or, 'I ate something that is making me uncomfortable.'
- Modifying – 'I'm not really depressed, just a little down in myself.'
- Suppressing – 'What I'm feeling is ridiculous; I'm just going to ignore it.'

All of the above defensive responses will result in the emergency feeling increasing in frequency, intensity and endurance in order to bring attention to the real movement that is being called for. It is critical that you seek whatever support is needed to take the necessary authentic actions that will reinstate well-being. When welfare feelings become your more frequent and persistent feelings then the emergency feelings have achieved their goal.

The Power of Anger

Next to the welfare feeling of love, the emergency feeling of anger is perhaps our most important ally in safeguarding the well-being both of ourselves and of others. Anger is a very powerful emotional alarm, warning us of the existence of some threat and giving us the energy to take corrective action. Many people have major difficulties in expressing anger in a mature way. Some are too terrified of the feeling even to acknowledge that they get angry, while others are too forceful in their expression and attempt to control others through their anger. Those who suppress their anger employ passivity and people-pleasing strategies to appease their own or another's angry feelings but, because they do not use the energy of anger to express their needs, beliefs, worth and grievances, their well-being remains neglected. Equally, those who express their anger through verbal or physical aggression do not move forward but remain stuck in a vicious cycle of dependence and enmeshment in relationship.

Unfortunately, it is often the case that our different holding worlds do not make it safe for us to use our anger in mature ways. One of the primary obstacles to the mature expression of anger is that it is often rejected as bad or harmful. Certainly, anger is a powerful emotion and it is imperative that we find ways of being responsible and mature in its expression. A good starting point is to distinguish it from aggression. Anger is a feeling that arises spontaneously from your wisdom – you cannot control its arising – to alert you to dangers to your well-being. You deserve to deal with these dangers; otherwise there will be neglect in your life and that neglect will rebound on any relationships you have with others. While anger is a feeling, and feelings cannot hurt another, aggression – verbal or physical – certainly can. It needs to be acknowledged that the mightiest weapon of all can be the tongue; hostile criticism, ridicule, scolding, put-down messages, sarcasm and cynicism are some examples of verbal aggression that cause much human hurt and suffering. But these are aggressive actions, not anger.

It is not anger itself that gives rise to aggression but not owning the feeling. Anger is loving in its impetus; it is about your care and well-being. Anger creates the energy required to move us to champion ourselves or others. Without anger we would not have the power to stand up for what is fair, loving and respectful. Injustices and neglects that occur within the holding worlds of family, school, community and wider society would go unchallenged were anger to disappear. The essential message in anger is to take action for self (or for others), not action against another. When anger is seen to signal the need for action against another, then it is likely that it will lead to judgement, harshness, hostility and diminishment of the other's presence. This, then, is aggression, not anger.

Take the case of the client complaining of abdominal pain who, when asked if she expressed her anger, replied, 'Yes, all the time. I'm aggressive at work and frequently fly off the handle at home.' When asked if she showed anger to her mother, her response was, 'Oh, no. It would really upset her. She is the one who causes me to feel angry but instead I take it out on everybody else.' Her mother may not have been in a mature enough place to understand a sudden onslaught of anger directed at her but the truth in this mother–daughter relationship was that care of the daughter meant that she, not the mother, had to change. The client described her mother as 'perfectionistic', 'fussy', someone for whom 'you could do nothing right'. Yet she continued to visit her mother with the subconscious hope that some time she would receive approval and hence love – albeit conditional love – from her. Rather than remaining stuck with, 'She makes me so angry', this woman needed to take ownership of her anger as being there for her and to see the truth: she felt angry at herself for allowing her mother to rule her life.

Anger in this case arose as the power to help her move towards her independence, as the spur to do something about her untenable situation with her mother. By exploring the message of her anger she began to see that she needed to outgrow her dependence on her mother for approval; that she needed now to belong to, to approve of and to love herself so that she could live her own life freely and independently, in a way worthy of her. As the woman internalised and lived out this consciousness, her attitude towards her mother gradually changed. She began to see that her mother, for her part, did not belong to herself, that she had no sense of her own worth and, therefore, found it difficult to approve of others. As the daughter's own feelings of self-worth increased, she was able to give affirmation and affection to her own children, to her spouse and also to her mother, thus ending the conflict between them. This case shows that when anger is not used for the loving purpose for which it arises, then hurt and suffering ensue. However, when we respond to anger not by trying to get rid of it as if it were an enemy but by viewing it as a friend that tells us about our well-being, then peace in relationships will follow.

The mature response to anger has a number of dimensions:

- Value its presence.
- Own it as a message for you.
- Uncover the blocked need or violated value or human right involved.
- Determine the action needed for the need to be met or violated value or right restored.
- Take the required action for the self.

A typical situation in which anger arises is when another person judges you – for example, as 'useless', 'selfish' or 'uncaring'. The anger you feel is there to alert you to the threat to your presence, or to a particular self-expression, arising from the judgement. It is not your job to correct the defensive behaviour of the other – that is the business of the person making the judgement – but it is your job to assert your own worthiness of respect and your own dignity. This assertion may or may not involve communication with the other person. If you do feel the need to engage with the other, your assertion might take the form, 'I do not perceive myself in those terms but I wonder what blocked need of your's lies behind your judgement of me.' Even though you are communicating in a mature way, the other person may still react unfavourably. You may need to assert your dignity again by saying, 'I am willing to listen to you when you're in a place to communicate respectfully but right now I am choosing to remove myself from your presence.'

The wisdom of our anger is perhaps easier to see when it arises in a situation where we witness a child being berated or violated in some way. We can readily recognise that children need adults to champion their worth and their right to safety in all areas of self-expression. The purpose of anger when it arises in this kind of situation is to move us to take action to vindicate the rights of the child and to restore any violated rights. Of course, our actions need to be assertive and definite but not aggressive or coercive. Regrettably, many children go without champions because the adults around them either are passive, not using the power of their anger, or aggressive, not owning their anger as belonging to them.

But it is not just children who need to be championed. When any human being – employee, neighbour, friend, partner, family member or manager – comes under threat, it is an act of maturity to stand up for their violated rights, and it is our anger that alerts us to the fact that something needs to be done. Championing does not mean taking responsibility for another but it does mean upholding your belief in the dignity of each person and your commitment not to stand passively by when that dignity is violated. Fear, along with anger, may occur when violations are present; your response will be determined primarily by your level of inner holding but will also be influenced by the level of safety present in the external situation. At times, it may not be safe to take action at the time of the violation; the wisest response may be to report the violation to the appropriate persons or to wait until the dust has settled and then confront the person who has perpetrated the violation. In these ways you use the energy in the feelings experienced.

The Power of Depression

In their book, *Depression: An Emotion Not a Disease*, the authors Michael Corry and Aine Tubridy describe depression as an emotion just like fear, anger or love. These authors believe that depression arises in response to stressful and/or traumatic experiences. They claim that in many cases a history of depression leads back to experiences such as bullying, sexual abuse or abandonment, and that these experiences have often begun in early childhood years. Our own work with individuals who feel depressed supports an understanding of depression as being purposeful and as having long roots in childhood. A person who exhibits depressive feelings inevitably experiences low self-esteem and despair that they will ever experience love. Acute depressive feelings can arise in response to the experience of overt loss – the loss of a loved one, a loss of status, the loss of a relationship, for example – but, when the depression persists, it signals a hidden and deeper loss – the loss of your own individuality. It is this loss that urgently needs to be addressed.

The purpose of depression is to alert you to the suffering that is present and to provide the impetus to resolve whatever inner and outer difficulties you are experiencing. Depression is a powerful ally, a messenger with crucial information on well-being and a window into what lies hidden and needs to be released. The deeper, more prolonged and more intense the feeling of depression, the greater the underlying level of repression of your individual presence and self-expressions. This can involve repression of your lovability, genius, emotional expressiveness and receptivity, capability, sociability, creativity and spontaneity. The challenge in depression is to accept its presence, to allow the pain to come ever further into consciousness, to receive it as a benign messenger and to get beneath the hollowness to what needs to be expressed and what actions for the self need to be taken.

Are Men Heartless and Women Loving?

When it comes to the issue of men and emotional expression and responsivity, several myths come into play:

- Men are emotionally illiterate.
- Men are heartless.
- Men live in their heads.
- Men have a one-track mind.
- Love is a woman's whole life; for men it is a thing apart.

If the preceding statements about men were to be true, then the essential ingredient for an enduring and deep relationship – being loving – would be missing and the predictions for intimate relationships, and all other relationships, would be dire.

It is easy to assume that those young men who, very tragically, take their own lives following the breakdown of a relationship are heartbroken. In fact, their tragic response to being jilted generally mirrors an inner breakdown of the relationship with the self. This inner alienation has its roots in the first relationships with parents, and perhaps also with other significant adults. The relationship such a young man would have formed with a partner is likely to have been of a lean-to nature. In such an enmeshed relationship security would have lain in his partner's desire for him, rather than in mature self-reliance. Heart is not present when you depend on another for happiness; what is present is the need to control or manipulate the target of your dependence so that she will be there for you. Aggression, controlling or dominating behaviour, hypercriticism, suicidal threats, sulks, hostile silences and violence are some of the defences that young, and indeed older, men can unconsciously employ in an intimate relationship.

Until men find heart for themselves they will struggle to have heartfelt relationships with others. It is common among men to reject the invitation to belong to self as being 'women's stuff' or 'soft stuff'.

When this response is explored, fears of being abandoned, laughed at, ridiculed or appearing weak emerge. Many wives, partners, girlfriends, daughters and mothers complain about the men in their lives not being emotionally available. What is often not appreciated by these women is that these men are not emotionally available to themselves. Until they are, they cannot be available to others. It is not optional for men to develop emotional literacy; it is a responsibility that, if not taken up, will have serious repercussions for all relationships.

If it is true that men have unconsciously learned that it is safer to be heartless, is it also true that women are more loving in their relationships with others? Certainly, the belief exists that women are more emotionally literate than men but this is not always borne out in their intimate couple relationships. Some common descriptions of women's responses in relationships with the men in their lives are 'over-emotional', 'emotionally distraught', 'histrionic', 'tearful', 'clinging' and 'all heart'. When women – as they have often learned to do – approach an intimate relationship with a man with the desire to please him, to look after him, to possess him or to be there for him, they too are being heartless in two ways. Firstly, they do not possess heart for themselves and, secondly, it is an illusion that they are being loving towards their men. It is not women's responsibility to look after the men with whom they are in intimate relationship; this is an unconscious means of attracting a man and the result is a lean-to relationship where the woman depends on the man for her security. When fear and dependence lie at the core of an intimate relationship, or any relationship, it is not based on unconditional love and, therefore, is without heart.

A truly loving relationship between a man and a woman is where the woman comes from an inner loving place and brings that emotional maturity to the man. She does not take responsibility for him but wants to get to know him in his fullness and so encourages his emotional expression. Feeling sorry for him is actually a heartless response, while believing that he can take responsibility for himself and for his feelings is loving. This is the relationship that is worthy of both men and women – one based on a solid 'heart-place' for the self and on self-reliance.

Is a Good Row Good for You?

There is a common belief that having a good row is good for you, akin to the notion that 'letting off steam' or 'getting it off your chest' is good for your health. The notion is that if you are 'boiling with anger' or 'seething with rage' it is best to release such emotional pressure. Similarly, it is often thought that when you are disappointed, hurt, fearful, upset, sad, or jealous it is essential you express these feelings. Venting anger, frustration or rage may reduce the threat of illness arising from bottling up such emotions but such venting can be seriously threatening to the well-being of another. In many adult relationships, in different settings, one person may be fearful or even terrified of opening up about unmet needs because of the possibility of an explosive response from the other party. Children learn to repress their emergency feelings when there is a danger of incurring the wrath of a parent, teacher or other significant adult. Where they have to bottle up their inner turmoil they often resort to speaking through their bodies – bed-wetting, soiling, asthma, stomach pains or frequent infections. It stands to reason that it is healthy to express how we feel and to communicate our unmet needs in the significant relationships in our lives but how that frustration or fear or anger is expressed is critical.

Feelings are always about the person experiencing them. Any person who believes that another person is causing her to be miserable, fearful, frustrated or angry, and blames or emotionally explodes, is not communicating effectively. Indeed, she is passing on responsibility for what she is feeling, which is a sure recipe for an escalation of her inner and outer conflicts. This is not to say that someone whose behaviour has been offensive, neglectful or threatening does not need to take responsibility for her actions. On the contrary, she needs to own her own actions and to uncover her own underlying insecurities.

Whoever reacts to such behaviour, however, also needs to follow the same processes of ownership and responsibility. It can be difficult to accept that our emergency responses to another's troublesome behaviour are signalling issues within ourselves that need resolution. You may wonder how it can be, for example, that when a woman feels fear in the face of her husband's aggressive behaviour her fear is not due to his aggression. In truth, her fear response arises from her wisdom and is alerting her to the fact that she is not strong enough within to be there for herself; her fear is crying out for her to deepen and strengthen her holding of herself. The woman who has a solid sense of her own worth and is highly self-reliant will be very definite in maintaining her own boundary in the face of her husband's aggression. She will let him know clearly and firmly that she does not respond to aggression and will only listen to what he wants to say for himself when he is ready to respect her presence.

In the above example, a crucial aspect of the woman's assertion to her husband is that he should speak for himself. When another person blames or judges you – for example, by saying, 'You're selfish,' 'You're heartless,' or 'You're a bitch' – she is attempting to get you to take responsibility for her, to read her mind and meet her needs. She is not in a mature enough place to communicate directly and clearly, and to take responsibility for her own needs. This does not mean that we cannot make requests of one another but there is a crucial distinction between making a request and being demanding and commanding. When you demand or command, unless the other person is in a place of inner solidity, it will be frightening for her to say no to you. On the other hand, a request provides the safety for the other to say yes or no, depending on her own considerations in the situation.

It can be seen, then, that having a good row is not good for you. Indeed, resolution of conflict is only possible when both persons involved take responsibility for their own feelings, own those feelings as being messengers about their own inner state, and take action for themselves in response to that inner state.

Professional Affectiveness

To be effective in what we do is something that all of us probably want. But what is often not appreciated, by men in particular, is that being affective is an essential aspect of being effective. The mind without affect is not mind at all. Equally, the practice of any life's work is not practice at all without heart. The two meanings of the word 'affect' are inextricably linked – affect meaning emotion is a powerful bedfellow of affect, meaning to influence.

A professional approach that is not affective in nature – an approach that does not encompass concern for each individual involved in a relationship – can act like a dark force in the lives of those exposed to it. Men have traditionally seen affective qualities as the 'soft' aspect of management; it is ironic how hard it is for men to embrace an affective approach in their professional lives. There is no mystery to men's resistance to being affective: males are conditioned by society into believing that showing emotion is a weakness. The truth, of course, is exactly the opposite – it is a profound weakness (in the defensive meaning of that word) not to be able to use the powerful information provided by your feelings. When professionals lead with both head and heart they themselves are far more balanced and, therefore, more effective. They then create an environment where others have a sense of belonging and feel safe and, as a result, are themselves more effective.

6. Communication – the Life-blood of Relationships

- Defining Communication
- Listening is an Act of Affirmation
- Listen, but Don't Personalise What You Hear
- It is Dangerous to Say what is Real
- What Others Say is About Themselves
- What You Say is About Yourself
- Identifying Defensive and Mature Communication
- Do Men and Women Communicate Differently?

Defining Communication

Communication is essentially about two things: providing opportunities for another person to get to know you and taking opportunities to get to know that other person. What is to be known will be determined by the nature of the relationship and by the particular circumstances involved. For example, in a manager–employee relationship it is critical that the manager recognises the individuality of the employee but the knowledge he needs will be about such things as work skills, attitude to work, commitment, psychosocial readiness to receive and give feedback, work needs, training needs and support needs concerning any personal difficulties that may interfere with work responsibilities. The employee also needs to recognise the individuality of the manager and, along with that, to know certain things about him, such as his style of management, his attitude to management and to the work organisation, his responsiveness to grievances, his commitment to fairness and his commitment to upholding the dignity of each employee. But in an intimate relationship and in the parent–child relationship there needs to be much deeper revealing of self and each person needs to get to know the other in a much more profound way. The desire to know the other needs to be non-judgemental, genuine and sincere. When this is the case, each person in the relationship feels comfortable about revealing his inner thoughts, beliefs, values, wishes, dreams, hopes, fears and needs.

In all relationships, your first responsibility is to know yourself. When that knowing is not present, it is not possible for you to get to know another or for another to get to know you. In order to know yourself, you must be able to listen to yourself and be in communion with yourself. This, indeed, is the key to communication with another; the nature of your communication with another will always reflect your own level of inner connection. Effectively, all communication is about union with self, a knowing of self, and a mind-and-heart conversation with self. If painful experiences in your life story have led you to become disconnected within, then any communication with another will be defensive in nature. You will resort to communication from the outside in rather than from the inside out. When the other person's way of communicating is similarly defensive, then communication remains conflictual. It is only when one of the parties to the relationship begins the process of internal dialogue that there is a possibility of a shift from defensive communication to open and authentic communication.

Listening is an Act of Affirmation

Human beings have developed, and continue to develop, amazing channels of communication – non-verbal, oral, written, face-to-face and through messengers like other people or technology. What is often forgotten is that listening is the first act of communication and this demands face-to-face (or at least to ear) contact. Indeed, there is nothing more effective than face-to-face listening. When you have the ears to hear, the eyes to see, the touch to feel, the heart to empathise and the head to understand, the possibilities in a relationship are endless.

It is not uncommon for people to find social interactions threatening and to find it difficult to start and maintain a conversation. For these people, it can help to remember that what most of us need in company is someone to listen, empathise and show interest in our presence and our lives. People who are good at listening are not very numerous, despite the fact that active listening is the basis of meaningful contact.

Active listening involves listening with both mind and heart and demonstrating spontaneous physical, social and emotional responses to what another person is saying. Active listening not only takes note of what is being said verbally but also pays attention to the array of non-verbal messages that accompany the words – for example, tone of voice, facial expression, mannerisms, body posture, eye movements and affective state. Furthermore, if you actively listen you also listen to the self, by observing your own internal and external reactions to what the other person is saying. Although self-listening is necessary so that you stay in tune with what is happening within yourself, you do not allow this information to distract you from your focus on the other. You may mentally note something you will need to consider later on, or you may wait for an opportunity to voice your reactions but not at others' expense.

The experience of another not listening to you can be very painful. Take the case of the man who at the age of four had the sudden realisation that his mother never listened to him. Four-year-old children need to ask many questions in order to understand the complex world in which they live; as a reaction to his mother's behaviour this man just stopped asking. In his mid-thirties he still had many questions that needed answering; but, most importantly, he also needed to listen to himself.

Some of the more frequent behaviours that block listening include the following:

- Wanting your turn.
- Moralising.
- Judging.
- Advice giving.
- The 'me-too' syndrome.
- Anxiety.
- Feeling resistant to the other person.
- Feeling frightened by what the other person is saying.
- Fatigue.
- Being preoccupied.
- A distressed inner state.

Wanting your turn in the conversation is a very common obstruction to listening. You can find yourself not being able to wait and not allowing the other person the time or opportunity to expand his ideas. Such behaviour springs from your own insecurity and your dependence on others to feel seen and heard. When you find that strong urge to get your turn, you know you are not ready to listen and that you are unlikely to be a source of support because you are not really getting to know the other person.

Moralising and judging are both attempts to impose your own values on the other. Not surprisingly, they are guaranteed to dry up any spontaneity and sharing from the other party. An example is the woman who went to her GP seeking help for her failing marriage and her confusion around her attraction to another man, only to experience being quickly put in her place with the response, 'Your place is with your husband and children'. Needless to say, she did not return to this medical practitioner.

There is a wise rule of thumb for listening to another: never give advice unless it is requested. Even when your opinion is asked for, it is better to offer suggestions rather than definite advice. Giving advice is putting yourself in the position of knowing what is best for another person – which you never can – and carries an implicit criticism of the other's ability to find his own solutions and conclusions. Those who constantly give advice often have an addiction to being needed.

The 'me-too' syndrome is another common communication stopper. The person supposedly listening really only wants to talk about himself and, no matter what the other says, will find a way to relate it back to himself with comments such as, 'Let me tell you about my experience', or 'You think you've had it bad . . .' Generally speaking, people who slip into 'me-too' responses are seriously insecure about being heard. Until this is resolved they are unlikely to become effective at active listening.

Feelings such as anxiety, fear or resistance make it very difficult to listen to another. For example, if you are anxious about an upcoming job interview it can be very hard to listen to someone telling you about an experience they had at work that day. When you find yourself in a situation where some emotional state is getting in the way of your listening, it can be helpful to acknowledge your feeling – if only to yourself – and let the other person know you are finding it hard to listen. Then, at least, the other will have an understanding of where you are in yourself and may even be able to listen to and support you in your emotional state.

If there is turmoil or distress in your inner world it can be very difficult to listen to somebody else's story. At one point in the life of one of the authors, he felt bitter and angry over the death of someone he had loved dearly. He carried that inner distressed state into company, so that he was not able to listen to or empathise with any of the others in the group. A good friend suggested that he would be better off being on his own and not inflicting his distress on others. The friend was right – what he needed at that time was to listen to himself and work through his grieving process.

Listen, but Don't Personalise What You Hear

If your partner says, 'You never listen to me', an important question that needs to be answered is: is he talking straightforwardly about his relationship with you or is he unconsciously talking about his relationship with himself? The answer to this question will not only determine what action is needed (or not needed) on either your or his part but will also influence the progress of the relationship between you. Even more crucially, the answer to the question can have critical consequences for the progress of each party's self-reliance and well-being.

If you – the receiver of the message – personalise the message and react to it as a judgement and a criticism, you are likely to respond defensively – for example, 'How dare you say that about me?', 'That's not true', 'Nobody else thinks that', or, 'It's terrible I'm like that' – and the resultant conflict will close down communication and add to the unhappy situation. Clearly, personalising the other's message is not helpful. If you can stay separate from the statement and hear it as being about something going on in your partner, then you can respond wisely by returning what has been said to him: 'What leads you to say that?' You have then kept the communication open and given yourself a chance to get to know your partner better. He may retort quickly with something like, 'Because you don't ever listen'. It may be true that you do not listen to him but it is important that that issue is not confused with his need to be listened to. In the communication between you it is important that the responsibility to let you know what he wants from you stays with your partner. He is the one who knows what he means by, 'You never listen to me', and he needs to communicate that understanding to you.

When the above instance of communication is examined within the context of each person's relationship with self, it emerges that the major responsibility for the sender of the message is to listen to what is going on within himself and to communicate from that inner place. Your responsibility is to stay separate and not to personalise his communication so that you can continue to listen to and understand him. The main questions your partner must ask himself are: 'If I feel that I'm not being listened to, what's that like for me?'; 'Why am I putting up with this, and what action do I want to take for myself?'; 'Am I putting up with it because there is a deeper non-listening going on within myself?'; and, 'If I was in a safe place to consciously hold and express my wholeness, wouldn't I have communicated a very definite message from my self to my partner – that I listen to myself and, when she does not listen to me, I assert my position and take due action for myself?'

Certainly, your partner can send you a clear message about himself and say, for example, 'I'm asking to be listened to when I speak'. I can easily listen to a request; it is not a demand or a command like, 'You have to listen to me', or 'I insist you listen to me'. These latter responses would put the responsibility for action regarding your partner's unmet need onto you, which is something you cannot accept for the sake of your own well-being. Your partner's request is an expression of the fact that he is listening to himself and that he would like the same kind of attention from you. In turn, you now have a responsibility to check in with yourself and to ask yourself how you feel about his request. If, in listening in to yourself, you find that you are not in a position to respond to his request – for example, because you are tired – you need to communicate that openly. Your open communication deserves to be respected without judgement, complaint or criticism. Of course, if you do not take on the responsibility of trying genuinely to hear your partner's experiences regarding listening in the relationship and if, following mature invitations to discuss the situation, you are not ready to respond openly to him, then he must follow through on listening to himself and take whatever action is needed to uphold his dignity and well-being.

Our responses to others spring not from our relationships with them but from aspects of the inner relationship with self, which need conscious examination. As long as you believe that your responses are about your relationship with another, your focus stays outside of yourself and the inner, mature path of self-reliance is not travelled. A pertinent question at this point is: if your responses to another's behaviour are about your inner relationship with the self, what, then, is a relationship with another all about? Essentially, relationship is about appointing another the guardian of his own ability to take responsibility for the self; this shows belief in the other and supports self-reliance. It is as if to say, 'I trust you to know what is happening in your inner world and I trust your ability to let me know about it. Equally, I want to be trusted to know what is going on in my inner world and for my ability to communicate this to you.' In this environment of mutual support of the other's potential to be self-reliant, expressed needs are much more likely to be responded to effectively. The key issue is that mature responsiveness to another's request does not entail taking responsibility for the other; rather, it involves a genuine choice about the request. Authenticity in relationship means being able when necessary to say no to a request but also being able to communicate the no in a way that reflects your own inner world. For example, you might say, 'Right now I can't listen to what you're saying because I need first to look after some unmet needs of my own.' If your partner can understand that your no is about your inner relationship with the self, he will be able to acknowledge where you are and repeat his request at another time. Both of you, then, are held in the relationship and can return comfortably and without threat to your own relationships with the self. There are now grounds for feeling optimistic about the mature progress of the relationship between you.

The above considerations apply not just to intimate relationships but to all relationships, in all holding worlds – for example, between parent and child, teacher and pupil, employer and employee, manager and staff member or medical practitioner and patient. These are considerations to which we need to return again and again in order that we may move from the more common lean-to relationships to relationships where each person takes responsibility for himself and supports that maturity in others.

It is Dangerous to Say what is Real

Often, one of the hardest things to do in relationship is to be real, to be authentic and to say what you truly feel, think and need. Being real never involves talking about somebody else. Rather, it means talking about and taking action for yourself. There are those who believe you should say straight out what you feel and think about another but if, for example, you bluntly call your partner 'stupid' or 'a controller' you are not being real; you are being defensive. Any time we send a 'you' message, we are hiding what really needs to be said about ourselves. In the examples above, the real message might be, 'I'd like my opinion to be listened to, at least', or, 'I'd prefer to make my own decisions on this issue'.

What is it that makes it difficult for us to be real? The answer is that it can be dangerous to be real. The greater the threat, the more unlikely it is that you will risk speaking your truth and the more likely that you will hide it under a defensive shield. Children learn the defence of inauthenticity early on when they experience the pain of rejection and punishment when they do not conform to the demands and expectations of parents, teachers and other significant adults who either dominate and control or are passive and over-protective.

Certainly in the case of children, unless they can find some adult who will champion their cause, conformity is the safest option in the face of threat. Adolescents frequently attempt to find support in being real from their peer group; this often gives rise to emotional storms within the family. Adults cannot afford to wait for others to make the world a safe place for them to be true to themselves; but unless you have found a fairly solid place of self-acceptance and separateness from the slings and arrows of others, you are more likely to continue to conform to the ways and expectations of those who threaten your well-being. Such conformity makes for deeply unhappy relationships and, unless one of the parties to a relationship finds the solid inner place from which to speak his truth, the relationship will continue to deteriorate. Conflict will continue to escalate in an attempt to wake you up to the unresolved issues that lie hidden within yourself and between yourself and the other person.

When past attempts to 'talk things over' have been met by another person with threatening responses – such as verbal or physical aggression, hostile withdrawal, unrelenting silence, screaming or threats to leave the relationship, to hurt himself, to commit suicide, to resort to alcohol or to swallow tablets – then it can be wiser to say nothing. However, saying nothing does not mean doing nothing; on the contrary, urgent action is required in such dangerous situations but it needs to be taken in a way that does not increase the danger to self. One definite action you can take is to break the silence on the threatening situation with a person with whom you feel emotionally safe, who will listen, be discreet and be non-judgemental and who, on request, will be able to suggest sound directions to take. Having such support may help you to determine ways of confronting the other party about your unhappiness in the relationship. Some possible strategies are as follows:

- Write to the other person.
- Give the other person an audio recording of your concerns.
- Request that the other person talk to someone he respects.

If there is no positive response to such overtures, stronger measures are required. Actions always speak louder than words but you need to be sure that you take such actions within your own level of safety and within a climate of unconditional regard for the other. Remember that it is the behaviour and not the person of the other that is challenging. Some possible actions are as follows:

- In the case of an intimate relationship, move to a separate bedroom or safe refuge.
- In the case of a manager at work, take sick leave and ask a medical practitioner to send a letter to the relevant department, consult with your union or file a complaint with the human-resources department.
- Break the silence on the threats with experienced people who can offer support and advocacy.
- Keep a record of any violations experienced.
- Seek counselling yourself so you can become more empowered.
- Seek the advice of a solicitor.
- Where there is intimidation or violence, report this to your medical practitioner and to the police, seek refuge and obtain protection from the legal system.

Taking actions such as the above may exacerbate the other person's defensive responses; such reactions are an attempt to deter you from continuing your assertive stance. It can also happen that compensatory responses emerge – for example, weeping and promising all sorts of changes – once you retreat from your decisive actions but these behaviours are also defensive in nature. The best proof of change is sustained effort to respond to your unmet needs. A particularly good index of another's willingness and readiness to be more mature in a relationship is agreement to attend counselling. A refusal to reflect means there can only be a short-lived respite from the defensive behaviours causing the distress in the relationship.

What Others Say is About Themselves

In a situation where your behaviour is being criticised or appraised in some way, maturity in communication can only be held when you interpret what the other is saying as being about him and not about you. For example, when service users comment on a service provider's practice it is crucial that such feedback be taken as a message about the service users' unmet needs and that an attempt be made to explore how such a situation has arisen within the service user–service provider relationship. If the service provider hears the feedback as being about his practice he has gone into the defensive position of personalising; he may now either retreat into himself and become anxious, or attack and become aggressive about the feedback. Either way, he has effectively broken off communication with the service users and is not now in a mature enough position to inquire more deeply into their experiences of the service.

In our clinical experience, it has become clear that each client experiences the therapist differently and that each client needs a different therapy. Thus, it would be very unwise to depend on any one client's feedback on our practice to feel confident about what we do. Were we to do so, our confidence would be steady one day and shattered the next. Confidence in our work is our responsibility and is a separate issue from any individual client's particular needs. If we were dependent on a client's positive feedback to feel good, or if we feared criticism from clients because it made us feel bad, then we would not be in the mature place of separateness that allows us to listen to and hear what clients say about their individual and particular needs.

The results of a recent survey of service users' perceptions of the Irish child-protection system (by Helen Buckley of Trinity College Dublin) serve to illustrate the necessity for separateness in good practice. Among the seventy service users surveyed, the feedback was split 40 per cent/60 per cent in terms of positive to negative feedback.

The central issues in the negative feedback were as follows:

- Social workers were seen as powerful, unsympathetic and hostile.
- Users felt they were not taken seriously.
- Users experienced harsh and unfair judgement.
- Users were given too much responsibility too soon.
- Users had concerns about future services (especially for children and teenagers).
- Users experienced delays and unreturned phonecalls.
- Users felt abandoned.

The key elements of the positive feedback were as follows:

- Users valued the practical and therapeutic help received.
- Users valued the understanding experienced.
- Users valued the kindness and calmness experienced.

It would be interesting to know whether individual social workers received both negative and positive comments from different users. It is quite likely that they did because the responses of each individual service user reflect that person's own inner world and are determined by his own level of self-esteem and empowerment.

If we consider the negative feedback as being about the service users then the comments noted above could be reflecting unmet needs such as the following:

- A need for empowerment, empathy and kindness for the self.
- A need to take their own situation seriously.
- A need to find compassion within themselves for the unhappy situation being experienced.
- A need to be empowered to request further help.
- A need to connect more with the self and to pursue determinedly the fulfilment of their needs.
- A need to possess and be there for the self.

If the focus is put on exploring the underlying needs involved in these comments rather than following the distraction to the service providers that would arise from personalising them, then practice could be greatly enhanced and it would be much more likely that unmet needs would be addressed.

Whilst it is not critical for the service users' sake to discover the hidden messages underlying their positive comments, it is important for the service providers' practice that they understand that these comments, just as much as the negative ones, reflect the service users' inner worlds. When clients show appreciation for 'the practical and therapeutic help received' they are voicing the inner experience of being able to receive and act on the help they have got, and they may need to show appreciation of their own contribution to the therapeutic endeavour. When they report the experience of 'being understood', they may be speaking about how they have internalised the understanding given and the need to give themselves credit for this process. When clients report experiencing 'kindness and calmness' they may be reinforcing their own sense of these qualities within themselves.

Regrettably, in this particular case, the response of the Health Service Executive has been defensive. It has failed to receive the feedback as an opportunity to get to know more about the individual stories of service users so that services can be more readily geared towards their expressed (albeit indirectly expressed) needs. To respond to the clients' comments as if they are about the competence of social workers seriously misses the point. The competence of social workers is an issue for the social workers themselves. They need to be given support and encouragement to reflect upon it continually, according to standards of quality that they have established as being worthy of them.

What You Say is About Yourself

If you accept that what others say reveals something about them, then it follows that what you say reveals something about you. The latter may be a hard pill to swallow. When someone says, 'You're awful', and you realise that this statement says nothing about you but says much about the person making the criticism, then it is relatively easy to say, 'I'm happy to leave that judgement with you'. If you are concerned about the inner source of the judgement, you might feel easy about asking what would make the person say such a thing. But what about the case where you are in the defensive position of making a judgement about another person? How easy is it to accept that your judgement reveals something about your inner world?

Communication can change radically for the better when you begin to own the fact that your communication – verbal or non-verbal – always reveals something about yourself and never reveals something about the other person. For example, if you find yourself saying to your manager, 'You're such a bully', can you own the fact that, even though the manager may bully you, your statement is totally about you? The inner source of your statement is that you do not wish to expose yourself to bullying behaviour. The challenge is accepting that the statement 'you're a bully' masks the truth of what you really want to say and that the person who is neglecting your well-being is yourself. If you were in a solid and separate place, you might instead state, 'I do not respond to bullying behaviour but I will be responsive to mature communication'. If your manager were to react with further defensive behaviour, a possible response would be, 'I'm not going to expose myself any further to this bullying and, if it persists, I will take the matter further'. It can be seen that when we own what arises in us there is an automatic shift from the 'you' message to the 'I' message.

You may ask: what about the manager's bullying behaviour? There are two separate responsibility issues here. One is that it is the employee's responsibility to possess, or to develop, a very definite boundary in response to the manager's intimidating behaviour; the other is that it is the manager's responsibility to reflect on his behaviour and its sources within his inner world so that he does not bring whatever inner turmoil he may be experiencing into the relationship with his employee.

Identifying Defensive and Mature Communication

Defensive communication describes the situation where you either blame another person and attempt to get him to take responsibility for you, or blame yourself and take responsibility for the other. The defensive strategy of 'passing the buck' is clear in such statements as the following:

- 'Your place is here with me.'
- 'You do as I tell you.'
- 'You're useless.'
- 'You have to agree with me.'
- 'You're driving me mad.'
- 'You can't do that.'
- 'You're being abusive now.'

Examples of the protective strategy of 'taking the buck' of responsibility are statements such as the following:

- 'I feel so guilty for not being here for you.'
- 'I feel so bad that you're upset.'
- 'Other people's needs should always come first.'
- 'I'm sorry for bothering you.'
- 'I'm so useless – no wonder you're so mad.'
- 'I live my life for my children.'
- 'I'll always put my work first.'
- 'I wouldn't let my workmates down by being off sick.'
- 'I'm glad I got all my students through their exams with good grades.'
- 'Don't worry about me; what is it that you want?'

It is important to notice in the above statements that, while a message may begin with the word 'I', what follows is not necessarily a true and authentic 'I' message. A true 'I' message reveals that the speaker owns and takes responsibility for everything that arises in him; there is no question of taking responsibility for another, nor of getting the other to take responsibility for him. Some examples of real 'I' messages are as follows:

- 'I made that mistake and I'll correct it.'
- 'I am requesting a meeting with you.'
- 'I am experiencing a problem in my relationship with you.'
- 'I accept responsibility for this job and will do my best to carry it out.'
- 'I am not willing to take responsibility for nor to cover up another person's mistakes.'
- 'I apologise for losing my temper and next time I will try to communicate my needs more clearly and directly.'

- 'I'm very pleased that you have responded to my request to tidy your room.'
- 'I'm glad for you that your efforts in studying have paid off in good grades.'
- 'I really appreciate that you're listening to me; it was difficult for me to bring it up.'

Another useful way of becoming conscious of how you are communicating is to examine what you say according to the following four dimensions:

- Direct and clear – 'Mary, I would like to talk about the e-mail you sent this morning.'
- Indirect and clear – 'Somebody has sent me an e-mail and I really want to discuss it.'
- Direct and unclear – 'Mary, what the hell is going on with you?'
- Indirect and unclear – 'E-mail is the source of all my troubles.'

The direct and clear message is mature communication and comes from a solid 'I' place. The indirect and clear message is defensive, its indirectness arising in regard to the 'who' of the communication. The reluctance to speak directly to the person involved may be masking a fear of authority figures caused by a history of distressing experiences with significant adults such as parents, teachers, priests or medical practitioners. The defensive ploy at work is to eliminate direct communication so that the possibility of re-experiencing old painful rejection is ruled out.

The third, and most common, dimension is direct in the sense that it addresses the person involved, but it is unclear about the real message. This type of communication will have unconsciously evolved from a history of either harsh responses to or active neglect of expressed needs. The hope in the defensive strategy is that the other person will detect what the speaker really wants, without his having to take the perilous risk of saying it openly.

The fourth strategy is likely to be totally confusing for the person receiving the message. Firstly, it is impossible to know who specifically is being targeted in the communication; secondly, there is no clue as to what the sender's real need might be. An exploration of the life story of any person who engages in this protective strategy will reveal experiences of great threat to his presence and many, if not all, of his self-expressions. The indirect and camouflaged nature of the message is designed to ensure that there is no exposure to possible rejection, criticism or humiliation. This person's inner world is very dark; considerable safety, encouragement and support would be needed if he were to move out from behind such powerful defences.

Another way to explore the defensiveness or otherwise of your communication is to consider the emotional tone of the message being sent, along the following lines:

- Judgemental – 'You're stupid.'
- Controlling – 'You do as I tell you.'
- Strategic – 'You're such a pet – you'll do that for me, won't you?'
- Superior – 'I know what's best for you.'
- Neutralising – 'You'll feel better in the morning.'
- Certain – 'Make no mistake about it, I'm right.'

As for all defensive communication, the above messages are cleverly designed to offset the possibility of further hurt. Their aim is not, as is often thought, to confuse others but to protect against the recurrence of the old painful experiences that took place when the person risked being open and real in the past.

When you operate openly from a solid sense of self, the six types of defensive communication above become transformed into their opposites:

- Non-judgemental – 'I wonder how it is for you having failed that examination.'
- Permissive – 'I have no doubt that you can find your own solution to the difficulties you are experiencing.'
- Spontaneous – 'I would love to have a talk about some needs I have from you.'
- Equalising – 'I'm really interested in having your opinion on the matter.'
- Empathic – 'I hear how sad and down you have been feeling.'
- Tentative – 'This is my reading of the situation; I'd like to hear your view.'

It can be seen that whether your defensive communication comes from a 'Live your life for me' place or an 'I'll live my life for you' place, when you choose to move in the direction of authentic communication the resulting real message is similar; arising from separateness and responsibility for self.

Do Men and Women Communicate Differently?

Gender differences and male/female stereotypes have been the subject of many popular books, among them John Gray's *Men Are from Mars, Women Are from Venus* and Anne Moir's *Why Men Don't Iron*. It is in the area of verbal communication that these books propose an essential difference between men and women – women are more verbal than men; women talk more about people, relationships and feelings, while men talk more about things and facts; women use language in a co-operative way, whereas men use it competitively. Arising from these supposed differences is the notion that men and women routinely fail to communicate with each other. Other writers talk about men being 'hard-wired' – operating from the head – and women being 'soft-wired'

– operating from the heart. Some backing has been given to these notions from the observation that young men often have difficulties talking about their inner turmoil and that dark silence can lead them to take their own lives. But this hypothesis can be quickly countered by the fact that, compared with their young male peers, young women are five to seven times more likely to self-harm from a place of unexpressed depression.

A recent book by an Oxford professor of language and communication – Deborah Cameron – determines to lay to rest the simplistic idea that when it comes to communication men and women are essentially different. Cameron shows convincingly that the difference in language use between men and women is statistically negligible. For example, contrary to the myth, neither gender interrupts more than the other, neither is more talkative or empathic in conversation, neither is less assertive or poorer at verbal reasoning. To drive home her point that we should be wary of claims that men and women are very different when it comes to communication, Cameron cites the case of the claim in a popular science book by Louann Brizendine, *The Female Brain*, that women utter 20,000 words a day while men manage only 7,000. This claim turned out to be unsubstantiated and was quietly deleted in a subsequent edition of the book. While debunking the myth that men are from Mars and women are from Venus, and demonstrating that both are from Earth, Cameron poses the important question as to why the Mars/Venus myth is so popular, particularly among educated women in western society, when it would seem that such women have nothing to gain from such stereotypes. Surprisingly, Cameron concludes that when it comes to communication both men and women 'haven't a clue'. But there is unerring intelligence in human behaviour and if women are holding to the myth of inherent male/female differences then there is good reason to do so. Whilst there is no evidence of inherent differences between men and women in ways of communicating, there are very definite differences between the two in regard to power positions in our society. This is evident in many areas – religion, politics, high finance, leadership and management positions. Certainly, the gap is closing in some of these areas but the challenge for women to play a greater role in them remains. Until there is real equality between the sexes, both men and women will attempt intelligently to exploit mythical gender differences and sexual stereotypes as a substitute means of finding or maintaining power.

Present difficulties in communication, not just between men and women but also within the two gender groups, are traceable to the early relationships of each individual, where it became unsafe to engage in genuine, authentic, direct and clear communication. Communication arises spontaneously from our interiority. When our interiority is dark and insecure, communication will automatically reflect that inner turmoil; when we possess a solid interiority our communication will be open, sincere, direct and clear – except, of course, in situations of high threat to our well-being. When the nature of the relationship within an individual changes, relationships between people change. It is personal maturity that determines effective communication. All of us, both men and women, need to come down to Earth and find union with the self so that communication with others will promote union between people. This is a major challenge in a world of great threats to being true to self.

The Unspoken Secret of Communication

We want to conclude this chapter on communication with speaking the unspoken secret that no matter where you are or whom you are with, everything you exhibit, verbally and non-verbally – your tone of voice, bodily posture, facial expression, eye-contact – reveals your inner world. The examples below illustrate the point:

- Failing to listen – disconnection from self.
- Listening actively – connection with self.

- Not interrupting while listening – solid and calm interiority.
- Interrupting while listening – inner blocks to being authentic.
- Being judgemental – little inner self-regard.
- Not judging – solid sense of self.
- Being superior – hidden feelings of inferiority.
- Being controlling – poor self-control.
- Being permissive – belief in self and others.
- Neutralising – repression of certain emotions.
- Being empathic – emotionally in tune within.
- Speaking with an angry tone – at odds with self.
- Not making eye contact – no sense of 'I'.
- Having a severe facial expression – little kindness within.

The opportunities are present at any moment for all of us to deepen our maturity of communication. The more the heads of our different holding worlds make it safe for us to be true to ourselves and to take responsibility for all our communication, the more the maturing process will be accelerated.

7. Relationships Interrupted

- All Relationships get Interrupted
- The First Interruption: Disconnection from Self
- Types of Interruptions
- Stories of Interrupted Relationships
- When is Enough Enough?
- Preventing Relationship Interruptions
- Separateness Prevents Against Interruptions
- Knowing the Self Prevents Against Interruptions
- Others Knowing You Prevents Against Interruptions
- Knowing the Other Person Prevents Against Interruptions

All Relationships get Interrupted

It is inevitable that over the course of any relationship there will be interruptions. Interruption is not an all-or-nothing affair. An interruption can vary from a relatively minor disagreement, where the interruption is mild and temporary, to a situation where the interruption is so great that it is better for the two people involved to bring an end to the relationship – for example, when one of the parties is exhibiting persistent and serious aggression. Interruptions occur when one or both parties go into defence, exhibiting substitute behaviours like acting in, acting out, addictions or illnesses (see chapters one and nine). The level of defence determines the seriousness of the interruption. The extent and duration of the interruption reflects the interplay of the stories of the two people involved. Clearly, if both individuals are in defence it is very difficult to heal the interruption; it is really only when at least one person finds inner solidity that it is possible to re-establish open relating. Another important influence on the extent and duration of the interruption is the level of dependence of the person at the receiving end of the other's defensive behaviour. In the child–parent relationship, for example, it can be very difficult for the child to stay in an open place in the face of interruption from the parent. In an adult–adult relationship, however, if one of the parties is in a secure, independent inner place, then she will be able to respond to the interruption from the other by establishing firm boundaries that safeguard her well-being. Of course, even a mature individual will react defensively at times and cause interruption in the relationship but, once the dust has settled, she will take responsibility for the interruption and return to open relating.

Interruptions can occur in any of our holding worlds – in the womb, the home, the school, the neighbourhood, the workplace or in wider society. The perpetrator of the interruption can be a person of any age with whom someone has a relationship. It could be, for example, a mother, father, son, daughter, sibling, partner, lover, medical practitioner, teacher, friend, neighbour, relative, policeman, bank manager, accountant or boss.

The First Interruption: Disconnection from Self

Any outer intra-couple interruption masks, and also mirrors, a hidden interruption – the inner disconnection from self. The healing of the outer interruption is dependent on the healing of the inner interruption. For example, you may notice that your passivity in your relationship with your father is causing frequent interruption but you will only be able to relate to him harmoniously when you discover what inner fears prevent you from openly expressing your power. Disconnection from self has its source in a lack of unconditional holding in the first couple relationships of a person's life – between child and mother, and between child and father. If a child encounters further interruptions – through conditional holding – in other significant relationships, such as with child-minders, grandparents or teachers, then the disconnection becomes greater. The child, in her wisdom, manages the disconnection by creating substitute responses; later on, as a teenager and adult, these very substitute behaviours will themselves interrupt relationships with others. No change can occur unless the inner disconnection is resolved.

As an adult, no matter what interruptions you may have experienced in earlier or current holding worlds, the resolution of any disconnection from self now lies completely in your own hands. However, it is important to remember that the substitute responses you created to shield against the pain of disconnection from self were created at an unconscious level and resolution involves bringing into consciousness what lies hidden. An environment of unconditional love is the only one in which you can pursue such a process. It is a fundamental truth that interruptions within and without can only be resolved through the experience of unconditional regard – from another, perhaps, but ultimately from yourself. When your earlier holding worlds have been unsafe, opening up to unconditional regard is not easy. It is very difficult to trust in a relationship if, as a child, the most important people in your life did not love you unconditionally for yourself. The self is wise and will be slow to risk any recurrence of the unbearable pain of rejection.

While healing inner disconnection is challenging, it is a responsibility that each one of us bears. Until we at least start to do so we will continue to bring our substitute behaviours into our relationships with others and, thereby, continue to cause interruptions in those relationships.

Types of Interruptions

Interruptions can occur because of violations either to your person or to your expressions of self. In the former case, one kind of severe interruption, which has particularly grave consequences when it occurs in our early holding worlds, arises from the outright rejection, exploitation or violation of your presence. In this kind of interrupted relationship there is no way of gaining attention, either through your person or through your behaviour, and the substitutes that need to be found have to be very powerful if they are to offset despair. A second kind of severe interruption, which again has grave consequences when it occurs in our early holding worlds, arises from conditional loving. In this interruption you are loved not for your unique presence but for measuring up to some expectation on the part of the other person – for example, to be successful, good, obedient, quiet or hard working. In this kind of interrupted relationship there are at least behavioural ways of gaining some attention but there is no contentment and no peace because you are in constant fear of failing to measure up.

In the second type of interruption, the violation can involve one particular area of expression, or several; most usually, interruptions involve the latter. For example, when an adult hits a child, the interruption involves the invasion of the child's physical, emotional and behavioural boundaries. Physical violation always involves emotional rejection and, because it is usually some behaviour that provokes the physical violation, it means that a behavioural violation has also occurred. If the defensive behavioural correction was for a social behaviour – for instance, speaking out of turn in the classroom – there has been a social violation as well. If the defensive correction related to an intellectual activity – for instance, a reaction to a poor school report – the young person will also have been violated in her intellectual expression. In the work situation, where a manager bullies an employee, not only is the person of the employee violated but the emotional, intellectual, behavioural, social and creative areas of self-expression are also affected. Obviously, the more areas of self-expression are violated, the greater the impact of the interruption.

In order to provide some guidance in detecting the kind of interruptions to which we are all subject at times, and which we in turn visit on others, some examples are given below for each of the areas of self-expression:

- Physical – pushing, pulling, slapping, pinching, punching, violence with a weapon, demeaning comments on physical size and appearance.
- Sexual – inappropriate sexual touching, sexual vulgarity, punishing a child's sexual self-stimulation, forcing sexual activity, harsh rejection of sexual invitations, demeaning comments on a person's sexual attractiveness.
- Emotional – suppressing, mocking, ignoring, modifying, punishing, dismissing or displacing feelings, being blamed for another's feelings.
- Intellectual – labelling as 'slow', 'weak', 'stupid', 'average' or 'thick', confusing knowledge with intelligence, punishing mistakes, confusing success with intelligence, irritability or aggression when learning or working, comparing intellectual

expression with that of others, not affirming intelligence.
- Behavioural – perfectionism, intolerance of mistakes, rigidity, impatience, disappointment, aggression, having unrealistic expectations, having no expectations, over-protection, a lack of opportunities to explore potential, putting profit before people, bullying, not listening, passivity.
- Social – snobbery, superiority, ignoring a person's presence, diminishing a person in front of others, hypersensitivity to criticism, dependence, controlling behaviour, judging, gossiping, hostility.
- Creative – judging, making derisory comments, absence of affirmation, rigidity, enforcing conformity.

Stories of Interrupted Relationships

The stories below illustrate how interruptions of an ongoing nature always involve an enmeshment of defences on the part of the two people concerned.

In the context of the holding world of the family, a common interruption in the intimate couple relationship arises from a male partner's obsession with work. The man's substitute behaviour of addiction to work means that he does not give enough time, energy or commitment to deepening his relationship with his partner. Where there are children, he is not present to his children in the way they need him to be in order to feel safe in their world. In our work, many sons and daughters have told us how hurt, angry and disappointed they have been in their relationship with their father because in their experience he always put work before his relationship with them. In this situation it is not unusual for a coalition of mother and children to be formed as a defence against the seemingly uncaring responses of the father. Of course, the father will retaliate – often in an aggressive and argumentative fashion – that he is doing all this work for them; internally he will genuinely feel hurt and misunderstood by the members of the coalition, particularly by his partner.

The reality is that the father's addiction to work arises because he is confusing his sense of himself with work. Work has become his way of achieving recognition and, as with all addictions, it is extremely difficult for him to let go of this response. Indeed, until he has resolved the confusion and is on the way to unconditionally recognising his own worth, it is perilous to try and stop his dedication to work. However, the impact on his wife and children can be devastating. Many partners of such men complain about feeling used, neglected, pummelled into submission, abandoned, hugely disappointed and sick of hearing promises like, 'I'll change, I'll change'. These women often say that if it were not for the children they would have left the relationship a long time ago.

Certainly, the responsibility for children weighs heavily on many mothers' shoulders and becoming a single parent is not a desirable prospect. However, as for their male partners, there is a deeper reality that these women need to face – a reality that was there before giving birth to their children – their dependence on others. Unconsciously, these women look to their male partners as a substitute source of security and, in order to maintain this substitute security, they can be over-pleasing. The relationship is now co-dependent – interrupted – and will remain so until one or other finds inner solidity. The man faces the challenge of finding his unconditional regard for himself, while the woman is faced with the challenge of finding her security from within. Unless each parent reflects and finds a resolution for the inner disconnection from self, not only will present family relationships remain interrupted, but the children will probably also repeat either their father's or their mother's dependence and will bring substitute behaviours into their future marriage and family relationships.

In the context of the holding world of the workplace, a not-uncommon interruption occurs when an employee 'can't stand the sight of' her manager. When explored, this interruption often involves defensive behaviours on the manager's part – such as bullying, superiority, public demeaning, rubbishing of his employee's ideas or relentless and aggressive emphasis on targets. On the surface it might appear that the manager's actions are the sole cause of the interrupted relationship but the truth is that the employee's own substitute behaviours also play a role.

Take the case of the woman in her late thirties who told us how she hated and dreaded going to work every day because of the outrageous bullying behaviour of her employer. She saw him as being the sole cause of her misery. In therapy it was gently pointed out to her that as long as she blamed him and was waiting for him to change she would never find resolution. In exploring her own responses in the situation, what emerged into consciousness for her was that her father had been and continued to be violent, domineering and aggressively controlling; her helplessness around her employer was the helplessness she had necessarily and unconsciously created in response to her father's highly threatening behaviour. What had been repressed and needed to be brought into consciousness was her worthiness to be treated with dignity and the rightness of an assertive 'no' when she encountered any lessening of her presence. She also saw that condemning her manager was a way of keeping the spotlight off herself and of avoiding the challenge of upholding her dignity, self-respect and well-being. Resolving the interruption in this particular case involved resigning from her post and taking a case of bullying against her employer. Whilst she gained knowledge of herself from the interrupted relationship he, sadly, remained in the defensive position of blaming her and missed the opportunity to get to know himself better.

Another story of interrupted relationship involves a man who was made redundant after twenty years and experienced considerable depression afterwards. He told us of how he had always looked up to his boss and had worked tooth and nail for him over those years. He felt very much rejected when this boss handed him his redundancy papers. What emerged in the therapy sessions was that this man was still enmeshed with his father, still had a child–parent relationship with him and had continued to over-please his over-demanding father until that time. The father expected the whole world to revolve around him and, as a child, the man wonderfully assessed the situation and wisely conformed to it. As an adult in the interrupted relationship with his now ex-boss, he found resolution by bringing into consciousness his right to live his own life and to hand responsibility for their own lives back to his father and his employer.

Resolution to interruption in relationship is not always easy to find. Take the case, for example, of the daughter who felt that her mother totally depended on her. The danger for the daughter in asserting her right to a life of her own – such as, 'Mother, I love you but I need to fly the nest and begin to live my own life' – is that the mother may have had a very strong reaction, which would then lead to the daughter feeling utterly selfish and guilty. One young woman told of how, in spite of her mother's objections to her boyfriend, she determined that she would go to Rome to be married and would have two friends as the marriage witnesses. Her mother's response to this assertion was to scream, grab her chest and have a heart attack. The ambulance was summoned and the mother was rushed to hospital and into intensive care. The daughter never again mentioned the boyfriend or marriage – and the mother made a full recovery. In order for the interruption to be resolved, mother and daughter would have needed to disentangle their enmeshment with one another.

In the context of the holding world of community, people can often experience interruptions in their relationships with service providers such as banks, solicitors, medical practitioners and members of an Garda Síochána. Take the case of the man who, in his dealings with his bank, found himself interacting with a faceless representative who was either chiding him for missing a payment on an account or attempting to coax him into buying some financial product, without the context of a personal relationship or any knowledge whatsoever of the man's particular story. This man had been persistently challenging bank personnel to give thought to how they related to customers – and, indeed, to one another as colleagues – but was simply treated as an oddball.

In trying to resolve the interruption, the man firstly refused to engage in conversation with the faceless representative on the phone and requested that all matters be referred to his local branch, where he was well known and where he knew the personnel. The second action he took for himself was to decide that, if his request was not responded to, he would stop dealing with this particular financial institution. Experiences of depersonalisation in banks and other financial institutions, such as this man's, have wreaked havoc not only on our economy but also, even more seriously, on our emotional and social well-being in the holding worlds of community and wider society.

When is Enough Enough?

It needs to be accepted that there are times when interruptions to a relationship are such that the mature thing is to decide that enough is enough. All relationships, in all the holding worlds in which we live, need to be worthy of our dignity and, when they are not, difficult decisions may need to be made. Somehow this is easier – if still a major challenge – in holding worlds other than the family of origin, where we often fail to challenge what can be major disrespect for and diminishment of our presence. In our practice we have come across men and women who regularly visit their parents despite being met with hostility or crippling criticism or being ignored. The sons and daughters of such families often feel broken, wounded and emotionally devastated because of seriously interrupted relationships. For these parents the idea of independence, living your own life and being responsible for yourself cannot be countenanced. Any attempt to break free can be met with reactions such as sulking, hypercriticism, helplessness, aggression or histrionic behaviour. Often in these families the interruption arises from dominance, insistence on conformity and emphasis on education, achievement, status, public image or wealth; there is little recognition or affirmation of the unique presence of each family member and little demonstration of affection. When adult children return to this kind of family, they continuously feel wounded by the absence of any loving response. No matter how many times they return home, the talk will turn to the issue of achievements or comparisons will be made with a sibling perceived to be more successful.

Gross interruption occurs in a family where a child does not feel wanted or is exploited, mistreated or totally neglected. Returning to such a family, as an adult, results in the same darkening of the person's presence. Of course, parents never deliberately intend to hurt their children but nobody benefits from defensive responses – either passive or rebellious – to unloving behaviours. Each of us has a responsibility to belong to ourselves and to separate out from any person who lessens our presence.

When is enough enough? When can you solidly establish a boundary around your worth? When can you say to a parent, other family member, friend, employer or priest that you are no longer willing to be exposed to being neglected, judged, controlled or ignored? You may find that rationalisations pour out when you think of such a challenge – 'Blood is thicker than water,' 'I owe it to my parents – they brought me into the world,' 'What would people think of me?', 'What if anything happened to them?', 'I don't want to upset people,' 'People will see me as being difficult,' 'I won't be liked if I assert myself.' In these protective rationalisations we deny our own hurt and pain in favour of those who violate our presence. But there is a deeper, hidden issue behind the rationalisations – when we continually return to a hurtful relationship we have not yet come into acceptance and love of the self; we have not returned home to the self.

It is with the realisation of our own worth that we are enabled to make the difficult decision to remove ourselves from those who darken our presence – no matter who, when or where. Ironically, it is in asserting our right to dignity and respect that we provide an opportunity for those who neglect others to reflect on what causes them to act in that way. As long as any member of the particular holding world involved colludes and is passive in the face of depersonalising behaviours, there is no possibility for change for either party in the relationship. It is an act of love and care for the self and for the person who demeans our presence when we assert our right to dignity and respect; and it is an act of neglect not to do so.

What has been said of interrupted relationships within families is also true of interrupted relationships in any of our holding worlds – schools, workplaces, communities or churches, for example. The critical question to be considered in any relationship is whether it is worthy of our dignity. When our lived experience of the relationship does not respect our dignity and worth, then maturity calls out for serious decisions to be made. Equally, we need to consider whether our interactions with others are worthy of their dignity; when the answer is no then serious reflection and action are required from us.

Preventing Relationship Interruptions

While we can never prevent completely against interruptions in our relationships – because it is not possible for any of us always to stay in a place of inner solidity – there are four important processes that are powerful in helping us maintain open, harmonious relationships: finding our separateness from others; knowing the self; others knowing you; and getting to know the other.

Separateness Prevents Against Interruptions

As we have seen, it is when defence in one person calls out defence in the other that relationship interruptions occur. When you can stay separate from the other, when you can listen and not personalise what you hear, when you understand that everything the other says reveals something about her (see chapter six), when you neither take nor pass the buck of responsibility, then the chances are high that the other's defensive responses will not cause major interruption in the relationship.

One of the first steps to becoming separate is to leave the nest of the holding world of your home of origin. All the evidence suggests that if you remain enmeshed with either or both of your parents you are highly likely either to develop no relationship or an enmeshed relationship with a life partner or lifelong friend. These confused and enmeshed relationships with family members and significant others will also affect relationships in other holding worlds such as the workplace.

Separateness in relationships needs to start at the earliest possible time. This is particularly true for relationships between parents and children but also for other significant relationships, such as those between teachers and students, peers, sports trainers and players. Adults need to live their own lives, not to live their lives through others, and they need to create opportunities for each person in their charge to discover her own unique way of being in this world. The paradox is that the deeper the adult's own relationship with the self, the deeper the relationship with the other will be – whether that other is an adult, child or teenager – because the nature of the relationship will automatically be one of deep respect for the other's unique presence. When parents do not find their own separateness in their relationships with their children, it will be a major challenge for their children to fly the nest and to separate out from the enmeshed relationship with their parents. Sadly, when a young person does not manage to resolve this kind of enmeshment, she brings that inner conflict into her intimate relationships with others. Her ties to home will have a telling effect on any new relationship, whatever the setting – very often with sad and painful results.

Each of us as adults needs to reflect regularly on the degree of separateness we have attained in our relationships, because any enmeshment will inevitably lead to interruption. In order to assist you in such reflection, below are outlined twelve key indicators of separateness:

- Seeing the other people with whom you are in relationship as people in their own right.

- Seeing yourself as a person in your own right.
- Believing that parents, and all other adults, can take responsibility for their own lives.
- Respecting the values, morals and religious beliefs of others.
- Respecting your own values, morals and religious beliefs.
- Being authentic.
- Being self-directed, independent and self-responsible.
- Being spontaneous in the expression of your feelings, ambitions, wishes and needs.
- Being able to say yes or no to others with whom you are in relationship.
- Being caring in an empowering way when other adults are unable to do things for themselves.
- Not permitting interference or intrusion into your own life by other adults.
- Enjoying your privacy.

Knowing the Self Prevents Against Interruptions

Throughout this book it has been repeated that everyone wants to belong. We want to belong to a partner, a family, a group, a workplace, a community. It has also been said that the priority is to belong to yourself, to your own interiority; otherwise there is a danger of over-involvement, under-involvement or no involvement at all in your relationships with others. The nature of your relationship with another – whether harmonious or interrupted – is totally determined by the nature of your relationship with yourself.

The more you know the self, the more likely you are to be able to prevent interruptions and to deal effectively with them when they occur. In order to appreciate and relate to another in her individuality, you need to have a strong sense of your own unique self; to have a harmonious relationship with a unique other you first need to know your own uniqueness. It is in knowing the self that you find that human quality noted above as being essential to the creation of a fulfilling relationship with another – separateness.

Paradoxically, it is in our interactions with others that we have the most valuable means of getting to know the self. Our relations with others throw up all our vulnerability, self-doubt, fears and challenges and, if we can face these and reflect on what lies hidden beneath them, then we have the wonderful opportunity to understand ourselves better and find open, mature ways of safeguarding our well-being.

Strangely, the people you cannot stand provide the most powerful opportunities for getting to know the self. You may have people in your life around whom you feel highly uncomfortable, people whose company you cannot tolerate; while it can be very difficult for you if you encounter these people frequently, it is with them that you have an opportunity to become conscious of your own hidden vulnerability. One of the first things to understand is that it is not the person you cannot stand but some aspect of her behaviour. If you confuse the person with her behaviour and, as a result, label her as, for example, neurotic, sociopathic, attention seeking or ridiculous, you will have created an interruption in the relationship and the opportunity to understand the self more deeply will have been lost. (Certainly, you take action about a behaviour that is bothering you, but not against the person of the other. There is no doubt that when you separate troubling behaviours from the person exhibiting them it considerably eases the tension those behaviours cause.)

If, instead of labelling, you stay with yourself, then the reactions that arise in you when you encounter behaviours you cannot stand will become windows into the self. They will point, perhaps, to hidden areas of your shadow world that the trying behaviours are resonating with, or to unexpressed values that have not been upheld. The key question to consider is: what is it in me that is making it impossible for me to feel anything positive towards this person and their behaviour? If you continue to blame the other person for your reaction – 'He's such a bastard,' 'She's so full of herself,' 'He thinks he's so smart,' 'She's so downbeat' – there is no hope of resolving the tension in the relationship. You may find yourself, for example, in a situation where a work colleague's perceived nervousness, timidity and lack of confidence gets on your nerves; you consider yourself, by contrast, a 'doer'. When you take your reaction as being totally about you, you can begin the process of tracking what lies behind your reaction. It may be that behind your own go-getting behaviour you are frightened of touching into your own lack of confidence and insecurity.

The truth is that when you have inner security you will not be reactive to another's behaviour, although you may well be proactive. You are reactive when you judge, condemn and get irritated with another, while being proactive means that you stay separate from the other's behaviour without diluting the mature actions you may need to take for yourself. In the present example, if your colleague's timidity means that she is not carrying her weight, you may certainly want to ask her to do so in a way that is equal, respectful, direct and clear. From a place of reaction you might respond sarcastically to your colleague – for example, 'For heaven's sake, get the skids on!' – whereas if you are being proactive you might respond with, for example, 'Mary, I need you to keep pace with the work demands'.

Others Knowing You Prevents Against Interruptions

It also helps to prevent interruptions if you ensure that the significant others in your life know you; at least, that they know you in ways relevant to your particular relationship. The old saying, 'If you want to know me, come and live with me', appears to make a lot of sense but more often than not it is the shadow rather than the real self that is known by both parties to the relationship. In an intimate relationship, for example, if each person understands the other's life story, the chances of a harmonious relationship are far higher.

If, for instance, your husband knows that in your life story there has been a history of alcohol abuse – by your parents, for example – he is more likely to be proactive rather than reactive if you defensively try to control his drinking. In a teenager–parent relationship, it can reduce tension if the parent lets the young person know which of his needs are being met when he sets certain limits and boundaries around behaviour. In the classroom, a mature teacher will let her students know what she requires in her relationship with them in order to uphold her own dignity and self-respect. In the workplace, a manager who is mature will work at communicating aspects of herself that are relevant to her role – her belief in the power of the unique individual, her unconditional regard for herself and her employees, the boundaries around her managerial responsibilities, her openness to uninterrupted listening, her work expectations and organisational goals, her belief in justice and fairness. The more the two parties to the relationship know one another – whatever their particular relationship – the smaller the likelihood of interruptions.

The extent to which others know you is entirely in your hands; another person can only know you to the degree that you let her into your inner world. Any person who says, 'I know you better than you know yourself', or, 'I know what's best for you', needs to see and reflect upon her own defensive communication if she wants to maintain an uninterrupted relationship. Nobody can know you better than you know yourself; and if you want another person to know you then you are responsible for revealing yourself to her. If you expect the other person to read your mind, you have not taken on the responsibility to know and reveal the self. What you are doing instead is seeking a substitute way of knowing the self by passing that responsibility on to another. Often, in long-term intimate relationships, if one partner is in a situation where her needs have not been met she will complain to her partner, 'You should know me and what I want after all these years'. But it is not your partner's responsibility to know you; it is your responsibility. Certainly, it is a bonus when another person anticipates your needs, but ultimately it is up to each of us to communicate our needs to the people with whom we are in relationship.

Knowing the Other Person Prevents Against Interruptions

Just as the other's ability to know you is in your hands, you can only learn about another person to the extent that she chooses to reveal herself. It is sometimes thought that we can know another person from her non-verbal communication, her verbal responses and her actions but all of these are symptomatic of underlying or hidden realities. We can have no knowledge of these realities unless the other person invites us into her inner terrain. We can guess, make assumptions and form hypotheses but these will all be about us. Maturity means that we check whether our guesses, assumptions and hypotheses about another person have anything in common with what she knows to be the truth about herself. If, when in relationship with another – a parent, a teacher, a partner, a lover, a friend, a therapist, an employer, a garda or a priest – you find yourself judging, labelling, advising or dismissing the other's point of view, you are not operating from a solid interiority. You are operating from a place of ignorance about the other person and there will now be an interruption in the relationship. In order to re-establish the open communication that will enable you get to know the other person, you need to take back your projections, reflect on them and discover what you can get to know about yourself through that process.

We sometimes feel that we really do know another person better than she knows herself and that when she disagrees she is 'in denial' and should be made aware of her 'irresponsible actions'. We feel that we should insist that she examine what lies behind such actions and their effects on others. A typical example is the case of a person addicted to alcohol, whose drinking has negative effects on her own health and on the well-being of others in her life. But the 'kick in the ass' approach does not work. Instead, it causes interruption in the relationship, because those who are troubled and troubling to others have been hurt enough already. As outsiders we cannot know the source of these powerful defensive behaviours, which the person has created unconsciously to protect herself from re-experiencing tremendous hurts. Trying to get a troubled individual to 'face up to the reality' of her behaviour adds insult to injury. No one wants to stay stuck in the darkness of denial. The truth is that the troubled person will only be able to face her inner turmoil when she feels safe enough to do so. Only she knows exactly what dangers are involved for her in doing this and only she knows when sufficient safety exists for her to engage in the process.

The importance of each of the two parties in a relationship knowing each other's stories is highlighted in a recent memoir by Peter Godwin – *When a Crocodile Eats the Sun: A Memoir of Africa*. Godwin's seemingly quintessential English parents emigrated to Rhodesia, as it then was, before his birth and he was brought up in a world of English culture and values. All through his life, his relationship with his father was difficult. His mother often took on the role of mediator between the children and a father who was remote and emotionally inaccessible, and about whose life prior to Rhodesia the children knew very little. Towards the end of his life it emerged that their very English father was in fact a Polish Jew whose mother and sister had perished in the Holocaust. In the light of the father's story his remoteness and inaccessibility make complete sense. The double tragedy, however, was that by not being able to let his story be known, he and his children were deprived of a potentially warm, comforting, nurturing, healing relationship.

8. Individual Maturity Leads to Mature Society

- Society: A Collection of Individuals
- The Challenge of Individual Maturity
- Present Level of Maturity
- Blocks to Individual Maturity
- Confusion of Behaviour with Person
- Confusion of Fear with Love
- Confusion of Control with Love
- Confusion of Knowledge with Intelligence
- Confusion of Competence with Confidence
- Confusion of Wisdom with Maturity
- Fear as a Block to Maturity
- What Helps Individual Maturity

Society: A Collection of Individuals

How each one of us is in ourselves rebounds on all our relationships in the different holding worlds of which we are part. If our inner worlds are harmonious then we will be better able to live with one another in harmony. It is in this sense that individual maturity leads to mature society. Laws do not ensure our safety in our holding worlds. Laws, in fact, are a substitute response to a lack of love within and between people. And, like any other substitute response, they are necessary until real and authentic responses become possible.

The following story illustrates the connection between the nature of our inner worlds and our effectiveness in our outer worlds. As a child, a woman had unconsciously understood that in the holding world of her family academic achievement gained recognition and a sense of belonging from parents, who themselves had not had many academic opportunities. From adolescence onwards she had a brilliant academic career, always being first in her class, receiving awards and gaining first-class honours at university, and finally landing a prestigious job. But all her achievements had a hollow feel for her and the time came when she cast aside her brilliant career in favour of marriage and family life – much to the horror of parents, family members and colleagues. But for her the truth was that for the first time she felt full of life. For the first time she was making real choices for herself; for the first time the criterion for effort was no longer performance but a deep sense of secure well-being. The 'brilliant' career was not in truth brilliant. It was being lived by a shadow, and it was that shadow-self rather than the fullness of her presence that the woman had been bringing to her clients and her work colleagues. This shadow woman was not in a position to be truly effective and productive in her workplace and to give her clients the service they deserved. By contrast, her marriage and family relationships were harmonious, open and spontaneous, reflecting her inner state of realness and authenticity. She was very effective in creating a safe family holding world.

The Challenge of Individual Maturity

Since it is individual maturity that ultimately enables us to live safely, productively and harmoniously, finding our inner stronghold is a serious responsibility that none of us can avoid – not only for our own well-being but also for the sake of all those with whom we come into contact in our different relationship worlds. The mature processes of knowing the self and being self-reliant are the two vital issues that create inner and outer harmony. Thus human dignity, rather than an insecure dependence on laws, is securely enshrined in the relationships within and between individuals.

Maturity is about occupying your own individuality, being at home with yourself and knowing your own power beyond measure to take responsibility for yourself and for all that you feel, think, say, do and dream. This realisation of self is a long, complex, difficult and exciting process. It is a long process because of the repressions that have been in effect from your early years onward, and because of the development of protective strategies over many years. It is complex because it entails an understanding of and compassion for the shadow world of substitute behaviours you have created which, while being necessary, have hidden the light of self. It is a difficult process because it entails examining what is hidden and that can mean touching into deep hurt, pain, shame, humiliation, anger, rage, fear and terror. But the realisation of self is also exciting because of the gradual emergence of the amazing expansiveness and wholeness of your interior world, and the sacredness, uniqueness and giftedness of your presence.

The realisation of self does not involve changing any aspect of yourself or your behaviour. Your substitute behaviours have been developed for wise and compassionate purposes, and it is shadow behaviour in itself to attempt to eliminate them directly. Your shadow world of substitute responses is not the target for change. It has served you well and, rather, you need to embrace it. The challenge lies in realising, bringing forward into consciousness and expressing what has had to lie hidden for so long; not changing but emerging. In doing so, automatically, without intervention, the protective behaviours will begin to diminish and will eventually disappear. When you begin to bring forward what has been hidden, the now-unblocked light of self will shine out and radiate into your shadow world, slowly but surely dissipating the darkness.

In rising to the challenge of individual maturity, support – within yourself and from others – is very important. This is a journey that needs to be accompanied with great patience, compassion and kindness.

Present Level of Maturity

In considering the process of maturity, we re-emphasise here the distinction between the self and the different expressions of the self. The self is the pure consciousness that creates, directs and bears witness to all that occurs in our lives and cannot be reduced to any of the expressions available to it (see chapter one). As seen earlier, when the self protectively identifies with one of its expressions – for example, intellectual expression – this expression becomes a means to the end of substitute security rather than an open, spontaneous revelation of the self. When this happens, the self's explorations are boxed into intellectualism and the person loses out on the other dimensions of existence – physical, emotional, social, sexual, behavioural, creative and spiritual. Typically, even the intellectual expression itself becomes confined to a particular area within that sphere – academic achievement, for example – and the fullness of self does not expand beyond that particular frontier. Fear is the critical influence on whether you are open and spontaneous in your self-expression or whether your expression operates as a means to an end of substitute security.

An important aspect of exploring your level of maturity is to explore to what degree you are alert and open to all the different expressions of self available to you – and, indeed, to what degree you creatively apply that potential to yourself, others and the world. You may find, for example, that out of fear of the recurrence of old experiences of abandonment you have shut down your social, behavioural and creative self-expressions and have protectively created a shadow self that is shy, withdrawn, frightened, wary of people and nervous of risk taking. But, in examining this closing down, it is very important to understand that the self's creativity is always present. Although the creativity of presenting a shadow self – that is, creating a substitute way of being safe in relationship by being non-threatening – arises from the fearfulness born of rejection, it is just as powerfully loving as the creativity that arises from natural fearlessness. In our work we have come across many individuals who have created the most amazing protective worlds, defensive fortresses, hidden passages and secret rooms that powerfully hide the pearl beyond price – the self. We have come across fewer individuals who are safe enough within themselves to use their creativity to express their wholeness and fullness. This kind of creativity benefits all those who cross their path in the different holding worlds of which they are part.

How can we best examine our current self-expressions and determine whether they arise from fearfulness or fearlessness? Clearly, in the former case, the expressions will take the form of substitute responses, while in the latter case real and authentic responses will emerge. Certainly – and you will only be able to do this when you feel some level of inner safety – it can be helpful to notice, identify and perhaps write down what specific responses arise in you, as well as between you and others in your different holding worlds. One way of doing this is to take a few specific holding worlds, as is done in the example below, which considers the holding worlds of self, personal relationships, work relationships and the educational world:

Self	Others	Work	Education
Authentic	*Authentic*	*Authentic*	*Authentic*
Some sense of a spiritual dimension	Empathy	Responsibility	Enjoyment of reading
	Joyful response to another's achievement	Genuine desire to help	Enjoyment of educational programmes
	Appreciation of kindness shown		Appreciation of interesting lectures
Substitute	*Substitute*	*Substitute*	*Substitute*
Insecurity	Over-pleasing	Over-conscientiousness	Hatred of exams
Fearfulness	Worry about approval	Fear of risk taking	Doubt regarding intelligence
Dislike of yourself	Hypersensitivity	Lack of ambition	Tendency to hide opinions
Hatred of your body	No initiative	Fear of mistakes	
View of yourself as average	Tendency to blush easily	Unassertiveness	
Tendency to over-eat	Loneliness	Fear of work	
Failure to exercise	Failure to express needs	Tendency to work late	

When you are in a fearful place not many real and authentic expressions are possible. The intensity, frequency, persistence and endurance of your substitute responses will be proportionate to the level of personal suffering you have experienced in your life story. The effects of your substitute responses on others will be influenced both by their own internal state and the nature of the relationship involved.

Another way to examine your current functioning is to look at the following lists of some typical real and substitute responses and notice which ones turn up in your life:

Authentic	*Substitute*
Giving and receiving love	Being fearful of giving and/or receiving love
Being emotionally receptive	Being emotionally neutral
Being emotionally expressive	Being emotionless
Loving challenges	Avoiding challenges
Being open	Being closed
Being spontaneous	Being cautious
Enjoying time alone	Not being able to be alone
Having a sense of separateness	Being enmeshed with others
Being self-reliant	Relying on others
Being wholeheartedly involved in life	Being under-involved in life
Being decisive	Being indecisive
Having no fear of failure	Hating and dreading failure
Appreciating difference	Being threatened by difference
Being free to be yourself	Being afraid to be yourself
Listening to the self and others	Not listening to the self and others
Not conforming	Conforming
Being optimistic	Being pessimistic
Being flexible	Being rigid
Caring for the environment	Having no regard for the environment
Being independent	Being dependent
Having respect for the self and others	Not respecting the self and others
Taking responsibility	Being irresponsible
Being assertive	Being aggressive or passive
Being kind	Being unkind
Possessing self-control	Controlling/being controlled by others

Whatever profile of responses emerges for you, it needs to be viewed with compassion. The profile is a mirror of how you have coped with the kind of holdings you have been exposed to up to this point. The profile is neither good nor bad; it is just what it is. It is only by compassionately accepting where you are within yourself, between yourself and others, and between yourself and the world that you can deepen – or begin if you have suffered greatly – that ultimate and most important responsibility which is the holding of self. In the above exercise, you may also discover that your responses differ in different situations (for example, on a social outing, in the workplace or at home) or with different people (for example, a friend, your boss, your spouse, your father or your mother). These differences reflect the level of safety that is present – either enabling you to be truly and openly expressive of the self or leading you to mask what you dare not express (for example, truth, your own opinion, difference, separateness, individuality). If you are sometimes in a real place and you have some supportive figures and some safe situations in your life, you can draw on these in taking on the challenges raised by those persons and situations where it is perilous to be authentic.

Blocks to Individual Maturity

In reaching for maturity, it is helpful to be aware of the blocks to that process that turn up in our lives. Everyone encounters blocks to being themselves; these blocks arise from the substitute behaviours of others, particularly of parents, in our early lives – for example, impatience, irritability, failure to listen, aggression or passivity. Whilst it is never the intention of the person who is being defensive to threaten and hurt another, the reality is that threat and hurt do occur. The more dependent you are on the person who perpetrates the defensive responses, the greater the threat and the unconscious urgency to create a defensive response in return. In such a dependent relationship a circular causality operates: a defensive response on one person's part leads to a defensive response from the other. This cycle can escalate, sometimes to the point where very serious relationship interruptions come into play. When the priceless pearl of self is under great threat, the defensive weapon has to be equally great – even nuclear.

In chapter two we saw how the societal holding world has tended to keep secret certain truths about our true nature, and that this secrecy presents a powerful block to our human potential. The degree to which you have colluded with these secrets is an important barometer of the safety of the holdings you have experienced up to the present time and your consequent level of maturity. It is useful to check which of the secrets you have adhered to, and to what degree of intensity, and what aspects of your true nature you have had to hide. You may have hidden the following:

- Your genius.
- Your ownership of what arises in you and consequent actions.
- Your status as a creator (not a victim).
- Your ever-present understanding and knowing of the level of safety present in your life.
- Your individuality.
- Your ever-present self-reliance.
- The fact that you are unconditionally worthy of love in any conflict that arises between you and another.

Living is a totally different experience when you consciously operate from a confident place, where you are a genius and a creator, where you acknowledge that everything you feel, think, say, do and dream is totally about you, where you understand what gave rise to your ways of being in this world, and where you know that you are an unrepeatable individual, that you have reliably guarded the self and that your nature is unconditional love. These are our aspirations and, while we may not always achieve them, what counts is our intention and commitment to pursuing them so that we may express, ever more fully, our true nature.

Alongside the seven best-kept secrets, there are other blocks to self-expression, which we describe as creative confusions. Maturity may be described as a place of infusion where we have a conscious connection to our wholeness, to our unique presence and to our individual and powerful interiority. Confusion, on the other hand, can be seen as a creative substitute response whereby we cleverly go against (con) and mask aspects of our true nature by asserting an alternative reality to the true reality that is too dangerous to reveal. Children wisely pick up on the confusions manifested in adults' interactions with them and in turn take them on as realities, even though unconsciously they know – as do adults – that these are not the truth. Confusion exists when any of the following occur:

- An attribute or a behaviour is taken to be your identity – 'I love her – she's such a jolly person.'
- Fear is called love – 'It's just that I'm worried you won't look after yourself.'
- Control is called love – 'I'm making you do this because I love you.'
- Knowledge is called intelligence – 'He's the brainiest boy in the country – he got straight As in his Leaving Certificate exam.'
- Competence is called confidence – 'No wonder he's full of confidence – he's fantastic at his job.'
- Maturity is called wisdom – 'She's very wise – she never reacts to her manager's obnoxious behaviour.'

As you can see from the examples above, the essence of confusion is when our true nature – our unique presence, our loving energy, our intelligence, our innate confidence, our ever-present wisdom – is enmeshed with a condition, circumstance, expression or attribute.

Confusion of Behaviour with Person

One of the very strong messages that have permeated previous chapters is that 'I am not anything I do, say, think or feel.' Roberto Assagioli spelled out this distinction clearly:

- I have a body but I am not my body

- I have feelings but I am not my feelings
- I have desires but I am not my desires
- I have a mind but I am not my mind.

More could be added to Assagioli's list:

- 'I engage in behaviour but I am not my behaviour.'
- 'I engage in work but I am not my work.'
- 'I gain achievements but I am not my achievements.'
- 'I create relationships but I am not my relationships.'
- 'I attain wealth but I am not my wealth.'
- 'I experience failure but I am not my failure.'
- 'I experience success but I am not my success.'

When you protectively confuse the self with any circumstance, condition or expression, what emerges is a shadow self. As we have seen, the self is pure consciousness: it observes, it witnesses, it creates. The self is always present, even in the darkest of times. Its impulse is always loving and it is always directed at maintaining your well-being in whatever way is dictated by the existing level of safety in your life. Living becomes very painful when the self, in times of threat, has to identify itself with one or more of its expressions – for example, 'I am my body'. The cosmetics industry has thrived on this particular confusion and, in many ways, has contributed to the deep emotional pain that individuals experience when their appearance is critical to how they feel about themselves. Any respite from the fear of rejection gained by getting a beautiful body will be short lived. It is impossible to look perfect all of the time, and then there is the inexorable process of ageing. One of our responsibilities is to take care of, nurture, value and cherish our bodies, but it is essential that we do not become identified with them.

There are many individuals who will claim that they are what they feel. For them, when they feel depressed, for example, there is no space between the self and the depression. As a result, the depression is experienced as overwhelming. If the depression is seen not as who they are but as the outcome of their individual stories, then it can be understand for what it really is – a powerful means of gaining substitute recognition in unsafe holding worlds. There are individuals, too, who feel they have to be happy all the time and powerfully repress all emerging feelings of sadness, fear, upset or depression so that an image as a happy person is not shaken. In therapy, one of the main processes involved is to help a person who is distressed to get to the pure place where he realises, 'I experience depression but I am not my depression', or, 'I experience happiness but I am not my happiness'. While recognising the creativity and wisdom of this confusion, the identification of self with any particular feeling becomes a terrible constraint on the expansiveness of our true nature.

The confusion of self with work is very common, especially among males. A high percentage of men die within months of retirement, even though there may have been no sign of any physical illness at the actual time of retirement. Individuals who protectively find their recognition through work will neglect everything else – their own well-being, their partners, their children, their friendships – in the relentless quest to be acknowledged. Not surprisingly, these individuals do not offer mature leadership and management. Ironically, however, they are often the ones at the executive and managerial forefront in work, social and political organisations.

Success, status, power and possessions are further examples of passing conditions in life that can be confused with the essential self. Depending on the depth and intensity of the confusion, the consequences for relationships with others can be devastating. For example, when an individual is protectively power hungry and becomes leader of a country, the confusion of self with power can lead to the torture and mass murder of those sectors of the population that cause a threat to his power. Tragically, several examples of this exist in contemporary society worldwide.

A common confusion is the identification of the self with relationships with others. This is a confusion that is not easily overcome because it has its roots in earlier relationships with parents. Living through another or for another is a clever creation that arises when the self-relationship seems too perilous to pursue. The confusion is echoed in many songs, poems, novels and films. Songs such as 'I Can't Live (if Living Is without You)', 'You're My Everything' and 'You Were Made for Me' are frighteningly delusional. For example, a woman in an intimate relationship who subscribes to such confusion may experience threats of suicide or murder from her partner if she asserts her unhappiness and her intention to leave the relationship. Possessiveness, jealousy, control, aggression and the creation of fear in a relationship are all tell-tale signs of the confusion of the self with a relationship with another. Where there are children involved, inevitably the confusion of the parents is passed on to them.

Confusion of Fear with Love

It happens in many intimate relationships that one of the pair exhibits over-anxiety about the welfare of the other: 'Are you sure you'll be okay on your own?'; 'Don't drive too fast while you're away'; 'I'm anxious that you won't look after yourself'; 'Be sure you wear warm clothes'; 'Careful you don't hurt yourself'. All such messages, while they appear to be loving, in fact have the potential to undermine the confidence of the other person, particularly in the case of a child. The confusion arises from the idea that expressing fear for another's well-being is showing love and that, therefore, such behaviour should gain love in return. In the individual stories of people who subscribe to this confusion we have found that in their holding worlds they have unconsciously picked up the message that if you show concern and take responsibility for another – a parent, in the first relationship – then you gain recognition.

This recognition is of a substitute nature, but substitute recognition is better than no recognition. While this confusion continues, relationships with others are bound to be interrupted. The resolution of this creative confusion can be painful – we can, after all, get a lot of approval for this protective behaviour – but is ultimately utterly freeing.

Confusion of Control with Love

You are likely to recognise easily the relationship interruption that occurs from this confusion if you have ever been at the receiving end of a situation where another person is controlling, is giving advice, is dominating, as if you have no centre of gravity within yourself, as if without him you would be lost. This confusion of control with love is summed up in the oft-said statement, 'I'm doing this for your own good'. This is usually uttered while scolding, punishing or reprimanding. If truth be told, the person who controls in a relationship is doing it for his own good, albeit a substitute good. Out of fear of invisibility, the person who exhibits this confusion has unconsciously formed the strategy that says, 'If I control others, then I always will have their attention'. The substitute behaviour for you may be to acquiesce to the control in order to gain some semblance of the real experience of unconditional love for your unique presence. Behind the control and the threats is a person waiting to realise the wholeness of his being. Moreover, of course, those who acquiesce – who buy into the confusion ('Isn't he only doing it for my good?') – are also only individuals in waiting.

Confusion of Knowledge with Intelligence

The confusion of knowledge with intelligence has the very serious consequence of forcing people either to repress their vast intelligence or continually to put themselves under strain to prove it through the attainment of knowledge. Knowledge is one of the many wonderful pursuits of human beings; 102 different types of knowledge have been identified but there are not 102 different types of intelligence. The notion of multiple intelligences is strongly argued by Howard Gardner, and tests have been developed to measure different intelligences in individuals so they may be directed down the particular track that best matches their particular intellectual aptitudes. This notion takes no account of each person's individual story and results in his vast potential being boxed into specific knowledge areas. But why has this confusion of knowledge with intelligence emerged? And why is it so prevalent? The answer is an absence of unconditional love and a consequent search for a substitute means of gaining recognition.

Individuals deserve to be loved for themselves. They also deserve to have their limitless intelligence – as this is expressed in their amazing capacity to respond to their worlds – affirmed over and over, particularly in the early years of life. When adults hide their intelligence and come to believe that it is through gaining knowledge that you show your intelligence, they pass this confusion onto children. The sad fact is that this confusion results in much humiliation and a dread of learning. Some adults can take a superior position regarding others they perceive as being poorly educated but they are always on the edge of being knocked off their pedestal. The fact of not being educated does not mean a person is not intelligent. It usually means lack of opportunity and it can mean lack of motivation – the person may be more focused on other areas of his life. Science now suggests that each person is a genius but fear of ridicule and other threats still makes it terrifying for us as individuals to affirm an essential part of our nature – our vast intellectual capacity.

Confusion of Competence with Confidence

The confusion of competence with confidence is similar to the confusion of knowledge with intelligence. Typically, from an early age we protectively learn that it is 'cocky' to affirm quiet confidence about being able to master any particular task in any of the 102 areas of knowledge. We cleverly learn to enmesh confidence with competence and prove ourselves by the competence attained. Take the person who claims, 'When I can drive that car on my own, then I'll feel confident'. When asked what will happen if he has an accident after becoming confident about driving, he replies, 'I'll lose confidence'. Actually, the accident is an opportunity to increase competence. Confidence is a given which can neither be added to nor taken from, although it can certainly be hidden away. Taking on the challenges that face us as we progress through our different holding worlds is much easier when we have confidence in our ability to learn what we need to in any given situations. Fear of making a fool of ourselves, of letting ourselves down, of being seen as 'stupid' and of getting things wrong makes living a very difficult undertaking. Reclaiming our confidence from the shadow of fearfulness is one of the essential processes in becoming mature.

Confusion of Wisdom with Maturity

It may not be so easy to see how it can be a confusion to identify wisdom with maturity: we tend to associate wisdom with the sage, the mature person. But we are always wise. When we hide the light of our individuality, or when we mask our true identity behind veils of illusions, we are being wise in the face of threat – but not mature. The word 'mature' means 'full', 'ripe', 'complete'. It is a quality that lies at the end point of the processes of getting to know the self and becoming self-reliant. It is important that we understand for ourselves that our wisdom is always present. Even in what might be regarded as despicable behaviour there is wisdom – such behaviour arises from inner terror (and, sadly, can then create terror for others) and may be the only means available to a person to draw attention to himself and to the life of quiet desperation he is living. In recent times there have been several examples of young men committing mass murder in their schools and communities and leaving messages such as, 'I'll be known now', and, 'Now you'll see me'. One of the most difficult facts for us to accept is that when the light has been extinguished within a person, we are all in danger. For the sake of preventing such outrages, each individual must recognise and affirm the individuality of others. When we separate wisdom from maturity it becomes possible to see wisdom as always being present, even though maturity may be a long way off. Many protective behaviours may need to be dropped before we will be ready to embrace the profound difference between maturity – the expression of our fullness – and wisdom – the abiding knowledge of the level of safety existing in the worlds we inhabit, which leads us to adopt either real or substitute responses.

Fear as a Block to Maturity

Ultimately, as an adult, the blocks to a person's maturity lie within himself. They have been built up over many years in an attempt to ward off threats to his well-being from others – in the home, in school, in the workplace, in the community and in the wider world. The most powerful inner block is fearfulness – which metaphorically can be taken to mean 'fear of showing my fullness' – this being the emotional creation (see chapter five on Emotions Call for Motion in Relationships) that ensures that we do not engage in authentic behaviours that would put us at risk. As adults, we no longer have to be dependent in the way we were as children and teenagers. We can put a roof over our heads, provide for ourselves, look after ourselves, be separate and independent. But when we examine the number and intensity of the fears within, we realise that the task of becoming adult is not easy. Some typical fears are as follows:

- Fear of being alone.
- Fear of what others think and say.
- Fear of failure.
- Fear of success.
- Fear of conflict.
- Fear of the future.

- Fear of not being good enough.
- Fear of death.
- Fear of life itself.
- Fear of losing control.
- Fear of speaking in public.
- Fear of examinations.
- Fear of social engagements.
- Fear of being discovered as a 'fraud'.
- Fear of being criticised.
- Fear of being compared.
- Fear of performance appraisal.
- Fear of expressing anger.
- Fear of speaking the truth.
- Fear of confrontation.
- Fear of authority.
- Fear of being different.
- Fear of losing a partner or friend.
- Fear of the reactions of your father or mother.
- Fear of the reactions of a sibling.
- Fear of being judged.
- Fear of making a fool of yourself.

Fear necessarily and creatively cripples us. It prevents us from going forward because being forward was not given safe holding in our earlier lives. A crucial aspect of maturity is embracing fear as the ally you have created to reduce the danger to your presence posed by those people upon whom you were dependent but who were not in a position to guide you towards independence. Fear is not a weakness; fear is the strength that has protected you from further blows to your presence. Accepting this reality is the first stepping stone towards fearlessness – an emotional stronghold from which you can truly inhabit your own individuality.

When you examine the list of fears and note your own and how enduring and intense they have been, try also to note your power to begin to do precisely the opposite now. For example, the fear of being alone, of not finding a partner or of losing a partner needs to be countered by the reality that separateness – aloneness – is part of your nature and that you have all the resources needed to enjoy the depth and breadth of your own company. Indeed, comfort in your own 'al-one-ness' is the basis of a fulfilling and independent relationship with another person, no matter which kind of relationship is involved. What follows are examples of the kind of new responses needed in the face of each of the fears listed above:

- 'I love being alone.'
- 'What I think and say about myself is what matters.'
- 'I have joy in failure as a step in moving forward.'
- 'I have joy in success as expressive of my resources.'
- 'Conflict is creative opportunity for progress.'
- 'The future is in my hands.'
- 'Death is integral to life.'
- 'I want to embrace the moment.'
- 'I am always in charge.'
- 'I can express my truth no matter where I am.'
- 'I am not an examination result.'
- 'My presence matters no matter where I go.'
- 'I am not afraid to say who I am.'
- 'What another person says is not about me.'
- 'In a world of individuals, it makes no sense to conform.'
- 'I can listen to the needs of the person giving a performance appraisal.'
- 'Anger is a feeling – it can't hurt anyone.'
- 'The truth will set me free.'
- 'Confrontation is an act of caring.'

- 'Authorship of myself is what counts.'
- 'I embrace my difference.'
- 'Nobody owns anybody.'
- 'I am not responsible for my parents' defences.'
- 'I am not responsible for my siblings' defences.'
- 'A judgement is always about the person expressing it.'
- 'I am not anything I do.'

Rome was not built in a day, and neither will be the home of your adult maturity, of your fearlessness and expressiveness of your difference, truth and genius. Remember, though, that the creativity that, over many years, built the home of your shadow world is now available to you to bring forward the inner stronghold of self that has lain hidden.

What Helps Individual Maturity

None of us would be living in a shadow world if everybody around us – particularly those in governorship roles – were living in the enlightened world of self. But the reality is that we constantly encounter individuals who operate from a protective shadow world and cannot create the safe holdings necessary to foster mature self-expression. As we have seen, safe holdings are essential for the mature emergence of children's consciousness of self. Because children are in a dependent position, the absence of safe holdings means that children need to find substitute ways of being held. Adults who remain fearful and dependent on others need all the support they can get, from other individuals who can provide it, to free themselves of co-dependence. Finding such support is not that easy because within co-dependent relationships they will be strongly discouraged, and sometimes violently prevented, from seeking it, and because it is not often readily available. It is for this reason that there has been an unprecedented rise in recent years in the demand for counsellors, psychotherapists, psychoanalysts, family therapists and cognitive-behavioural therapists. This rise is supported by the prevailing attitude that individuals do not have to remain stuck in difficult relationships nor in the darkness of disconnection from self.

In seeking out the support of a therapeutic relationship, the most important factor to be considered is the nature of the relationship that is present between the person helping and yourself. You will recall that the seventh best-kept secret in society is that without unconditional love personal, interpersonal, organisational and societal conflicts cannot be resolved. Do not assume that because a person has professional training they will automatically create an unconditional relationship with you. When such a holding is not present – and this is true for all relationships – you need to move on. Everyone carries unresolved emotional baggage. It can happen that for one client a therapist has no difficulty in being unconditional, empathic and authentic, while with another it is a struggle to relate in that way. When the latter is the case the therapist has an opportunity to examine what in his unconscious is being triggered by the client's responses and is seeking to come into consciousness. It can help enormously if the therapist can be honest with the client about his inner struggle so that there is equality between the two people. Such honesty represents a return to unconditional relating and it may result in the client persisting with the therapy.

Of course, not everybody needs to see a therapist. Mature friendships, the modelling of maturity by significant others, courses on personal and interpersonal communication and effectiveness, inspirational reading, and support and encouragement from colleagues can often set you on the road to maturity. Whatever helps, avail of it and remember that support is a two-way street. People may say, 'I don't want to be burdening you with my problems'; the mature response is, 'I feel privileged that you have asked for my help. While it is you who need help today, it may be myself tomorrow.' Of course, in this situation a deeper issue is often also involved – the fear of re-experiencing dismissal or ridicule for talking about your problems.

From the foregoing it is possible to identify five facilitators of the pursuit of self-holding, self-expression and authentic self-reliance:

- Support, support, support.
- Being with individuals who model independence.
- Seeking environments where safe holdings are operational.
- Listening to and reading what is inspirational for you.
- Persistence, persistence, persistence.

The last is vital because the process of coming out of hiding can often be a case of one step forward, two steps back. Such regression arises from fearfulness within and the danger of other people's defences without. Recognising these ongoing threats helps to maintain persistent efforts to free yourself and come into maturity.

9. The Path to Individual Maturity

- Steps to Individual Maturity
- Unconditional Love
- Compassion
- Understanding
- Consciousness
- Emotional Attentiveness
- Responding to the Message of Substitute Behaviours
- Making New Choices and Taking New Actions

Steps to Individual Maturity

As we have seen, maturity is about coming into the fullness of your being; it is about realising your immense wisdom and power; it is about being self-reliant and inhabiting your own individuality. Finding maturity is the most important responsibility for each of us as members of society. This is not a benign issue that we can choose to dismiss, ignore or be cynical about; it is an urgent responsibility we have to ourselves and to all others with whom we are in relationship. We have seen that for those persons who occupy positions of governorship over others the responsibility of mature self-holding is an even more urgent matter because of the influence of their behaviour on those who are dependent on them.

The fact that our substitute responses are formed at an unconscious level does not give us permission to abdicate responsibility for how we are with ourselves and with others. On the contrary, when we become conscious of our substitute responses we also come to realise that these defences were created by us, in the face of threats to some or all aspects of our self-expression, and what we create we are responsible to. But we are not to judge, blame or reject ourselves in our defensiveness. Judging, blaming and rejecting are further defensive responses which indicate that, somehow, the pain of punishing ourselves for our actions is less than the pain of bringing into consciousness the abandonment we have experienced. The defences reflect the need for greater safety to allow what is unconscious to become conscious. In the meantime, we will necessarily remain in a protected place, but we must recognise the possibility that our protective responses – whether they take the form of acting in, acting out, addiction or illness – may pose dangers to the well-being of others.

In approaching the responsibility of maturity in our adult years, it becomes clear that our experiences in the first holding worlds determine the extent and the depth of the self-holding that now needs to be achieved. Those earlier experiences also provide an index of the level of danger experienced in regard to each of the areas of self-expression, and the degree and type of safeties that are now required for a raising of consciousness to occur. If in your life story your unique presence has been annihilated and all of your self-expressions have been met with harsh and violent responses, then it may be necessary to find a therapeutic relationship that will offer you profound holding of your presence and acceptance, understanding and belief in your self-expressions. It helps enormously when there is someone in your life who can offer support in your quest for maturity or can show the way on the self-holding odyssey.

Remember, if you had received unconditional love and belief in your immense potential in the first four holding worlds, then you would have gracefully progressed to the fifth – self-holding – and would no longer be dependent on others, even though you continue to live in different relationship worlds. Separateness in relationships is the hallmark of a person who occupies her own individuality; enmeshment or alienation in relationships mirrors the necessary and creative defences of being far distant from the self or of keeping yourself invisible.

In the pursuit of that inner stronghold of self, there are several key processes to be taken into account:

- Unconditional love.
- Compassion.
- Understanding.
- Consciousness.
- Emotional attentiveness.
- Responding to the message of substitute behaviours.
- Making new choices and taking new actions.

Unconditional Love

At the core of any mature relationship is unconditional love; without it the relationship is necessarily and creatively defensive and painful.

Unconditional love of self appears to be the hardest challenge to take on – not because we do not understand its essential significance but because it means asserting the unconditional rightness and worthiness of our unique presence. When in childhood our essential lovability has not been acknowledged by others, then open, unconditional love of self becomes a frightening, and even terrifying, prospect. In adulthood the dangers are still out there – for example, the dangers of violence, aggression, ridicule, dismissiveness, criticism, passivity, sarcasm, cynicism, judgement and castigation – and so it is no wonder that many people ignore or react against the challenge of loving and believing in themselves.

However, unless this unconditional regard begins to emerge, it is not possible for any fundamental change to occur in our inner worlds or in the outer relationship worlds that make up society. In chapter two it was pointed out that the seventh best-kept secret in society is that conflict – personal, interpersonal, occupational, educational, social or political – can only be resolved by unconditional love. Recall, too, that unconditional relating with self and others is not a 'soft' option; on the contrary, it involves having very definite and strong boundaries around your own dignity and the dignity of the other (see chapter four). There is a profound simplicity to the state of unconditional love: 'I love and accept myself, no strings attached,' and, from that inner conviction and free place, 'I love and accept the other person for her individual presence – no buts!' Unless the love that does not bind exists within, it is not possible – in spite of good intentions – to offer it to another. Unconditional love of self automatically leads to unconditional love of others.

Unconditional love is an infusion, whereby you operate from the solid interiority of self, where no confusions reign and where you are in a place to withstand the confusing responses of others. The most usual experience is that with some individuals and in certain environments you manage to stay separate – to withstand – whilst with other persons and in other situations you struggle to hold your solid ground and, at times, lose your foothold. These latter capitulations are not disasters. On the contrary, they are the signs of the need for further self-holding. The quest for maturity is a lifetime process that has its moments of ecstasy and moments of despair. What counts is to keep alive the intention to be true to self, to be real and authentic; it is a cause of great concern when the shadow world re-establishes its dominance and the intention becomes enveloped in darkness.

On the journey towards maturity, whether you are working alone or with a friend or therapist, patience is paramount. Our own practice has taught us that with individuals who declare a hatred of self, an abjectness, a profound sense of insignificance or a sense of being totally unlovable, patience has to be without limits. From our own lives and the stories of others, we have come to realise how extraordinarily difficult it can be for some individuals to allow themselves to feel loved; they are terrified to allow that possibility because they know the horrors of having love and regard withdrawn. Quite rightly, and creatively, they will test the love being offered in a therapeutic relationship and, in the face of such responses, the boundaries of the therapist often come under pressure. There are those (therapists among them) who believe that unconditional love is not possible, but there is little hope for peace on earth without the intention and practice of unconditional love. The key to the quest is not to confuse your own self with a behaviour, no matter how good, bad or outrageous, and to not confuse the self of another with a behaviour, no matter how benign or how threatening. It is in this separation of person from behaviour that there is clear space for the non-judgemental, compassionate and respectful response that is critical to the resolution of your own inner turmoil and that of others.

There is no greater tragedy than to have been forced to have recourse to alienation from self in response to experiences of abandonment in your various holding worlds. It is no easy task to cut the ties that have bound you to the threatening responses of others yet that is precisely what self-holding requires. Each of us is here to love the self and to live out your own unique existence, relying on yor own immense resources to do so. It is within yourself that you need to affirm your worth and immense potential – quietly, like a lover who whispers in your ear how precious, unique and sacred you are.

Individuals worry, and for good reason, that if you attempt to separate yourself from those persons with whom you have necessarily become enmeshed, you run the danger of being rubbished, blamed, judged and even physically violated. In such circumstances it is imperative to build up your own inner resources quietly, covertly to come home to self, and to affirm in silence all that you dare not express overtly. Finding support away from those who are threatened by your emancipation is crucial. The truth is that you can live without the enmeshed relationships that have been part of your life until the present time. Similarly, those who are dependent on you have the capacity to be separate and independent. It is of no service to yourself or to others to stay enmeshed; it offers an opportunity and an example for others when you are engaged in the most important human responsibility – being at home with the self.

The key affirmation for this process in self-holding is, 'Unconditional love is my deepest longing, and it is my due, and my responsibility as an adult, to reclaim that love for myself.'

The key action is practice of unconditional belonging to the self in the form of loving kindness for the unique being that you are.

Compassion

Sympathy, empathy and compassion can often be confused. Sympathy means feeling sorry for somebody, which can actually be a defensive response and patronising in nature. Sympathy does not empower and it certainly does not inspire responsibility for the self and for your actions. Carl Rogers has been to the forefront in emphasising that empathy is a core condition of psychotherapy. In essence, it means feeling with a person who is being emotionally expressive. Empathy is a genuine attempt to experience the emotional world of another in a non-judgemental way without interpretation and without neutralising her feelings. Empathy seeks to hold the expressed feelings of another so that that person can come into consciousness of what the experienced feeling wants to bring to the surface (see chapter five). Empathy towards yourself is an important response on the path to maturity.

Compassion includes empathy but also goes beyond it. Compassion certainly feels with the person who is suffering but also recognises that the suffering is an integral part of the human condition. It understands that a person's wisdom is always present and that love is always present at her core. Compassion is the heart's response to an individual's inner and outer turmoil and creates immense safety for the person who is suffering.

The key affirmation for the process of compassion is, 'All the suffering I have experienced and all the suffering others have experienced from my substitute responses truly deserve compassion'.

The key action is to embrace and consciously respond to your defensive behaviours and the suffering of others in the face of your defences, when consciousness arises of past and present hurts and pain.

Understanding

If compassion creates the emotional, physical, sexual and social safety for the acknowledgement and expression of suffering, understanding provides the intellectual, behavioural and creative safety for progression into the world of self. Earlier on (in chapter two), in the context of the best-kept secret that understanding is always present, we noted that individuals – therapists or others – who offer authoritarian interpretations of defensive responses do not recognise the power of the individual to understand and resolve her own psychosocial imprisonment. Be assured that no matter what arises in you, you know its source and you know the threats that caused you to create whatever substitute responses are present.

A good question arises here: how can understanding that is present but at the unconscious level help the consciousness that is vital to self-holding? Understanding at the unconscious level is calling for the safety that will allow what is below the surface to rise up. The task for the individual, or for the person in a helping role, is not to interpret but to provide emotional, intellectual, behavioural and creative safety. This safety will allow the emergence of the consciousness that, no matter how overwhelming the emotion, no matter how terrifying the behaviour, there are wise reasons for the presence of those experiences. The word 'understand' can be adapted to mean 'stand under': you need to go beneath your own or another's substitute responses and recognise, from the all-seeing position of the self, the frightening sources involved and the creativity that has been required to survive so many abandonment experiences. All defensive behaviour is created to guard the self. Its intention is not to threaten the presence of another but to reduce threat and to alert to the darkness within. The hope is that the flag of the symptoms being presented will not be flown in vain and that some mature person will provide the safe holdings that are needed so that the true self can come out from behind defensive walls.

The necessary intellectual and creative safeties are provided by the recognition of the intelligence (your genius – the first best-kept secret) that has assessed the particular dangers to self and self-expressions and has formed individualised and creative substitute responses to minimise the dangers (we are creators, not victims – the second best-kept secret). The required behavioural safety is provided through the acknowledgement that all behaviour makes sense and through the provision of opportunities for you to become conscious of your defensive behaviours, to make new choices and to take new actions.

Understanding is a safety you can offer yourself but if your shadow-self screens – either partially or completely – your real self, then understanding will initially need to be offered by another. In understanding defensive behaviours there is no attempt to dilute in any way the responsibility a troubled person has to the consequences of her actions. But, if understanding is absent – along with unconditional love and compassion – the consciousness needed for mature responsibility will be absent too.

The key affirmation regarding the process of understanding is, 'My defensive behaviours make sense, are intelligent and creative and are a window into what lies hidden, waiting to be revealed'.

The key action is the practice of 'under-standing' – getting underneath – your own and other individuals' threatening behaviours so you can uncover the real underlying issues that need to be responded to.

Consciousness

One of the core messages of this book is that much of what we feel, think, say and do arises from the unconscious and, unless what lies hidden comes into consciousness, no change in the direction of maturity can happen. In regard to our outward behaviour, it is often the case that we do not know its real origins and intentions and that we can rationalise our responses wonderfully. For example, we can justify violence by asserting, 'I was driven to it', justify passivity by claiming, 'It was not the right time to confront the situation', or justify work addiction by arguing, 'Somebody has to do it'. Possible hidden meanings in the above examples of unconsciously created rationalisations are: 'Violence is my one way of making sure nobody abandons me again', 'By not rocking the boat I reduce the possibility of further rejection', and, 'Without work I am nothing'.

You have also seen that a raising of consciousness is only likely when a relationship is unconditional, compassionate and understanding. These three processes provide the fertile ground for the roots of repression to shoot forth into conscious expression. Recall that it is not the behaviour you outwardly show that is the focus of your attention but the hidden expression of self that you do not show. Achieving consciousness is a two-pronged process – it involves, first, identifying your defensive behaviours; and second, discovering what it is that up to this point has been too threatening to express. This could be your individuality, your presence, your physicality, your sexuality, your feelings, your genius, your independence, your need to belong or your true creativity. Each of us has a two-sided story – an outer story and an inner story. It is what has been invisible in the inner story that needs to become visible, and this is the challenge that consciousness poses for us. What has been threatening to self and others in the outer story cries out for compassion and understanding.

The key affirmation in the process of raising consciousness is, 'I aspire to live my life from a place of consciousness of all that I am and all that I feel, think, say and do'.

The key action is to begin to identify, or be open to another pointing to, actions of yours that either harm yourself or threaten the presence or self-expressions of another. In identifying any particular defensive response – for example, always complaining of having so much to do – attempt to get underneath and uncover what needs expression. In this example, perhaps the underlying hidden cry is, 'I need to do a lot more for myself'.

Emotional Attentiveness

In chapter five we saw that feelings do not lie – they are always an accurate barometer of how you are internally at any one moment. Feelings arise, created by the self, as the precedents to action (or inaction). Being in touch with what is happening at an internal level is a crucial aid to the emergence of mature self-holding.

Early detection of emotion means early action; this action is always something we need to do for the self, not against others. When action against others occurs in response to emotion, you know that the defence of projection is present – the other has been blamed for your feelings. For example, anger arises and is detected and, rather than accepting the anger as a signal to take care of the self, you respond defensively by blaming other person – 'You must stop that – you're making me so angry!' Once the defensive response emerges there is a considerable obstruction to any consciousness of the need the feeling was signalling. However, when the necessary safeties are present, and you have internalised them, consciousness of the source and the real intention of the emotion will emerge. In the case of anger, the real action required may be for you to create a strong boundary around a particular self-expression and to say a firm no to any intrusion or attempted violation.

Similarly, when a feeling is acknowledged but then followed by an action against the self – often referred to as introjection – then what lies hidden will remain so until the necessary safeties become present. The action against self can be physical (for example, punching the wall), emotional (for example, telling yourself, 'I'm so selfish to be feeling like this'), intellectual (for example, telling yourself, 'This feeling is completely irrational'), behavioural (for example, swallowing some tablets) or social (for example, physically and emotionally withdrawing). These defensive responses pose obstacles to any further progression towards self-holding.

Even reading chapter five may very well have led you to deepen your attentiveness and to take progressive steps towards owning your feelings. Feelings are there so that, when there is psychosocial safety, we can reliably get in touch with what it has really been like for us in the past and what it is like for us in the here and now. Feelings tell us the truth about the holdings we have experienced and are experiencing in the different relationship worlds we are part of. For example, a woman who becomes conscious of being terrified of her male spouse and, with support, is able to hold and own her terror is likely to become conscious of another terror – the terror of standing up for herself that she carried as a child and teenager and brought into her marriage. She may also begin to realise consciously that her spouse's threatening behaviours are similar to those of one of her parents or of some other significant adult whose darkness impacted on her life. Further down the road of her emotional attentiveness and ownership of her feelings, she may become conscious that the deeper terror is within herself and that it is in reclaiming her own immense power and resourcefulness that she will be able to create the required boundaries around her presence in the face of others' shadow responses.

It can be seen from the above example that emergency feelings bring attention – when we are ready to give such attention – to the distancing from self that we have unconsciously created as a protective response to the threats to self and particular self-expressions we have experienced. With this recognition, there is a possibility of holding self and of uncovering whatever unmet needs the emergency feelings are signalling, and of creating new ways of responding that are heartfelt, respectful and committed.

The key affirmation for emotional attentiveness is, 'All my feelings make sense and are invitations to discover what is really happening in my inner and outer worlds'.

The key action is to be actively tuned in to emotions as they arise and keep attention on the feelings so that what needs to come to consciousness and what new actions need to be taken will follow.

Responding to the Message of Substitute Behaviours

As the tide of consciousness rolls in, you begin to notice the substitute responses you have developed in relationships with particular individuals, influenced in each case by 'who', 'what', 'where', 'when' and 'why'. It can be painful when you become conscious of your own dark responses and how these have affected other people's lives. Nonetheless, this is also a freeing and enlightening experience that can be used to lead you to establish mature holding of self and a consequent kind responsiveness to others.

In this particular process of reaching for maturity, do your utmost simply to notice, observe and identify your substitute responses – without analysis, judgement or rejection. It can be useful to note in a journal what comes into consciousness. Support yourself in this difficult process by honouring the fact that you are taking a monumental step in the direction of maturity. Stay aware of the fact that what may be deeply troubling and troublesome defences have been absolutely necessary for your survival. In consciously noting your substitute responses you may find it useful to use the categories described in chapter one:

- Acting-out responses (against others).
- Acting-in responses (against yourself).
- Addictive responses (to processes or substances).
- Illness responses.

It helps too to discuss and share your responses with someone who is compassionate and understanding. In this sharing, what lies behind the different substitute responses – what needs to be expressed and no longer repressed or suppressed – may be more readily realised.

Substitute responses are a window into all that you dare not express and so are *not* to be the focus of change. It is new actions – giving expression to the fullness of your own unique presence – that need to be the focus. Nevertheless, identifying and embracing your substitute responses will provide the means to get to what has been repressed and thereby determine the mature actions needed. Often you will find that the mature actions for self and others being called for are the exact opposite of the substitute responses that you have consciously identified. For example, the very common acting-out response of aggression may be calling out for the real response of asserting your worth, value and dignity. Similarly, the acting-in response of people pleasing may point to the repressed expression of your own relationship needs. An addictive substitute such as alcohol abuse may indicate that you have been swallowing down your anger and need to give definite expression to that feeling. Illness as a substitute may point to the real need to express the wellness of the self. There is wisdom in developing a substitute response that is opposite to the behaviour that was threatening for you to engage in, and may still be. The further away you are from the behaviour that led to rejection, the more you reduce the possibility of further hurt. In our practice we have come across many individuals who describe themselves as 'nothing' or as 'invisible'; the wisdom of such negations of self reveals itself when we find that somewhere in their story their presence was seen as a constant nuisance, completely ignored or even violated.

It can also be the case that your substitute responses point to projections on the part of a parent or other significant adult with whom you cleverly conformed because you understood unconsciously that to do otherwise would have been dangerous. For example, you may find yourself staying with a career that is not right for you because that was the career your parents chose for you and, because of fear of major conflict in your relationship with them, you dare not go against their expectations.

The saying, 'Friendship is God's apology for family', sadly often has real meaning when the support that will enable you to occupy the home of your own individuality is found with friends, not in the home of origin. The enemy of individual maturity is to be found in the substitute responses of others – for example, of parents, relations, friends, teachers, employers, managers, employees, members of the clergy or members of an Garda Síochána – but the task is not to vanquish the enemy but to remain steadfast in the face of threat, safe in the inner stronghold of self. Sometimes finding support can seem difficult but be assured it is out there. Remember too that those who are stuck in their shadow worlds are also looking for support, albeit still unconsciously.

In order to help you respond to the underlying message of your various substitute responses, some examples are given below of the kind of mature actions being called for:

Acting-out responses	Mature action called being called for
Being controlling towards others	Self-control
Being manipulative	Becoming spontaneous
Being hypercritical	Becoming affirming
Being harsh	Becoming kind
Bullying	Championing
Blaming	Owning
Destructive behaviour	Constructive behaviour
Being rigid	Becoming flexible

Acting-in responses	Mature action being called for
Passivity	Assertiveness
Shyness	Becoming present
Timidity	Becoming fearless
Perfectionism	Seeing your own perfection
Self-harming	Self-loving
Being compliant	Telling yourself, 'I'm here too'
Over-pleasing	Telling yourself, 'I am not my pleasing'
Being self-critical	Becoming self-affirming
Blaming yourself	Believing in yourself

Addictive responses	Mature action being called for
Addiction to work	Asserting your own worth
Obsession with getting things right	Discovering the rightness of self
Caring for others only	Caring for yourself and others
Worrying about what others think	Thinking well of yourself
Addiction to sex	Discovering the joy of being yourself
Addiction to gambling	Taking the risk of being yourself
Addiction to food	Nurturing yourself
Addiction to drugs	Coming alive to yourself
Addiction to alcohol	Expressing what lies hidden

Illness responses	Mature action being called for
Back pain	Turn back to self
Headaches	Getting to a heart place with yourself
Migraine	Becoming tolerant of difference
Irritable bowel syndrome	Resolving what is deeply irritating you
Digestion problems	Discovering what is hard to digest emotionally
Frequent infections	Giving yourself more affection
Diabetes	Being sweeter to yourself
Blocked arteries	Opening up your heart to yourself and others
Cold sores	Talking about what is sore for you

Making New Choices and Taking New Actions

New choices arise from the dawning consciousness of what has lain hidden and now dares to reveal itself. Consciousness of what lies behind our substitute responses tends to emerge slowly and to go from less threatening to more threatening revelations. For example, a person may come to consciousness that her fear of heights is about her fear of falling off a pedestal which, since childhood, she has had to occupy protectively. It may take a longer time, however, for her to become conscious that a fear of disappointing her mother, who had such high expectations of her, lies behind the pressure she has put on herself. Further down the line, consciousness will emerge about her overwhelming fear of expressing her own individuality and her right to live out her own unique life.

New choices need to be authentic in nature and are a call for action for the self and not against the self or against another – the latter kind of action would be a return to the shadow world. There is often a concern that focus on self will lead to individualism – a selfishness where nobody and nothing else matters except yourself – but this confuses individuality with individualism. In inhabiting your individuality you will automatically appreciate, accept and reinforce the individuality of the other. Furthermore, on taking responsibility for yourself you will automatically support others to take care of themselves; you will be the first to offer help and support to those not fortunate enough to be in a position to look after themselves. Individualism in this sense is quite the opposite of individuality. The former is a 'me, me, me' phenomenon, a narcissism that springs from a hidden feeling of invisibility and a deep insecurity; it is a creative response to felt invisibility meant to ensure, albeit in a substitute manner, that you are seen. Inhabiting your individuality guarantees mature responses towards yourself, others and the world, whereas individualism is a shadow response and needs to be challenged in an understanding, compassionate and unconditional but definite way.

We have seen the many different kinds of substitute responses that can give rise to the necessity of making new and authentic choices. Mature choices can only arise from a proactive place; any reaction is a return to defensiveness. Certainly, the emerging felt feelings of sadness, fear, depression, anger, rage, guilt or despair offer the opportunity for new choices but the required safeties need to be present for such choices to be put into action. The choices to be made are always particular to each person and her unique story up to the present time. When you manage to keep your attention on the emotions present, it is highly likely that the new directions being called for will begin to rise into consciousness.

Take the experience of the medical practitioner with a dread of speaking in public – a dread he shares with about 90 per cent of the population, although the source of the crippling fear is particular to each person's story. In the case of this individual, earlier in his career he had suffered a mental block when giving a talk to colleagues and had stumbled and stuttered his way through the presentation. Rather than examining the source of the mental block, he determined never to give another presentation. Avoidance was a certain means of making sure he did not re-experience the embarrassment, humiliation and felt sense of failure. However, a defence never resolves a fear and, twenty years later, he still had a dread of public speaking. He was encouraged to experience the fear fully, and what began to emerge was a fear of letting others down, then a fear of letting himself down and, eventually, a fear of letting down his parents, who were highly conscious of public image. Several new choices began to emerge for him – to be independent of what others thought of him, to embrace failure as opportunity, to create opportunities to practise public speaking, to separate his identity from his professional performance, to be spontaneous, and, finally – giving rise to the greatest challenge – to live his own life and cut the ties that bound him to his parents' projections onto him.

These are all worthy and necessary aspirations but living them was an entirely different matter. Once new choices emerged this man needed to remain conscious of his mature aspirations, schedule relevant activities and follow through on the decisions he had made. Support from within himself and from sources such as reading, audio recordings, lectures on self-empowerment, along with encouragement from his spouse, helped this man in his maturing process.

Very often individuals can be catapulted into seeing the light through the experience of a crisis – perhaps the death of a close family member, relationship breakdown, losing a job, serious illness, financial debt, witnessing the abuse of children or an attempted suicide by somebody close. The initial response to a crisis tends to be defensive – for example, 'Why did this have to happen to me?', 'Where did we go wrong?', 'I'm sorry I ever got married', or, 'It's best say nothing – it will only make things worse'. When the dust settles, and provided the support is there to examine how best to respond to the crisis, consciousness of what has been hidden will arise and new decisions will begin to emerge. This is especially common following a relationship breakdown, where each party has the opportunity to examine what emotional baggage was brought to the relationship and still needs resolution. When such reflection does not take place, inevitably the next intimate relationship will become as troubled as the one that has just ended. Serious illness leads many individuals to evaluate their lifestyles and to recognise their priorities. We have encountered several men who were addicted to work and who, following their heart-bypass operations, were ready to give more attention to care of themselves, to their marriages and to their relationships with their children. Suddenly work was no longer the panacea they had thought it to be.

From day to day it is important that we notice not only what we feel but also what we think, say and do. Noticing how our bodies are is also very necessary. Noticing is not the same as analysis. Analysis can often bring paralysis; noticing is an act of caring. When, for example, your thoughts and words are of an anxious, pessimistic, depressive, jealous, possessive or controlling nature, then it is an act of maturity to sit with them and allow what lies hidden behind these defensive responses to emerge. Similarly, when your actions lead you to rush, to fret, to act aggressively or to be passive, manipulative, controlling, hard-hearted or dismissive, you need to find the support to examine what lies behind these substitute responses.

Your body is also an ally and if you are experiencing recurring symptoms – for example, back pain, migraine, stomach upsets or insomnia – and have been diagnosed as having a stress-related condition, then your body is strongly signalling that you need to care for the self. Keeping a journal of your feelings, thoughts, actions and dreams can be a step in the direction of maturity, as can finding like-minded individuals who will support your worthy quest. When you feel stuck in a rut of defensiveness – in spite of your good intentions and efforts to be real – recourse to a psychosocial professional may be necessary. The likelihood is that major and unconscious terror of standing in the shoes of your own individuality is present and an equivalent level of unconditional love and a holding of all self-expressions are required.

10. The Power of Relationships

The nature of the relationships between people determines emotional, social and economic prosperity but it is the relationship within each individual that determines what happens between people. Does this mean, then, that our entire focus needs to be on individual maturity? Certainly, the primary focus needs to be on each person occupying his own individuality but the importance of the relationship between individuals can not be underestimated, not least because of the enormous pain and suffering such relationships can create, and because of the obstructions to the emergence of a mature society that ensue. Whilst resolution always lies at the individual level – a difficult and sometimes bitter pill to swallow – the couple relationship, the relationship between two individuals, offers two powerful means by which maturity may be deepened – support and conflict.

When relationships are of a supportive nature – wherein each party to the relationship shows unconditional regard, belief in the other, compassion and understanding, sets definite boundaries and models self-possession – then the progression towards a deepening of individual and societal maturity is accelerated. In a situation where one party brings a sense of his fullness to another, who is struggling with his own identity and manifesting strong defensive responses, the possibilities for a raising of consciousness on the part of the troubled person are high. It is in this way that each individual in his relationships with others can offer a foothold to those who are in the quicksand of fear – a foothold that will enable them to begin the inner journey of self-discovery and independence. It is good to see that, although the hiding of self and of self-expressions comes about in relationship with significant others, the emergence of self also occurs in relationship. It makes sense that if the original circumstances leading to repressions of self arose in key relationships, emancipation is best achieved in key relationships also – but, this time, relationships that offer unconditional safe holding.

As an adult, a key supportive relationship can involve a partner, friend, colleague, therapist or parent – anyone who has resolved, or is on the path to resolving, his own repressions. Whilst many health practitioners recommend that their clients attend therapeutic or personal-development groups, it is not the group that provides the support (indeed, the group situation can sometimes be experienced as highly threatening), but individuals. When the group is a collection of like-minded people, then the couple interactions that occur will be of an empowering nature. Some groups – such as families, workplaces and communities – can be deeply divisive, however, and the safeties needed for an elevation of consciousness are absent. Nonetheless, conflict always offers the possibilities of seeing what you have not dared to see up to the present time.

The creativity of conflict between people is that it is a manifestation of individual inner conflicts. Whilst conflict creates pain and suffering, it also calls for individual maturity to emerge. However, unless at least one of the two people involved finds some inner safety, the likelihood of conflict resolution is very low. When no resolution emerges, conflict necessarily escalates and so continues to knock at the doors of the repressions of both parties. When one of the parties begins to see what is occurring, the issues of conflict now become sources of revelation – revelation of what lies hidden and needs to come into the light. When one person becomes more enlightened, similar possibilities are present for the other person. Whether or not the other person avails of the opportunity, the nature of the conflict will change because one party now is operating from a place of consciousness. The person whose consciousness has been raised is now able to embrace the conflict as an ally and begin to examine what lies behind his defensive responses – such as passivity, helplessness, emotional withdrawal, manipulation or emotional outbursts. Thus, passivity becomes empowerment, emotional withdrawal becomes an emotional drawing closer to the self, manipulation becomes an active listening to and direct and clear communication with the self, and emotional outbursts become emotional attentiveness.

Because we are always in relationship – from the moment of conception to the final moment of death – it is necessary that we avail not only of the love and support that may be present but also of the conflict. It is not by hiding away in a monastery or taking yourself off to a mountain top that you best get to know yourself but in the amazing, colourful, exciting, painful and frightening relationships that you encounter. It is through relationship that you can best encounter who you are and bring all of that unique potential and power to others – thereby creating a better world for yourself and for the people around you.

One of the points strongly expressed in this book is that systems – family, work, religions, governments, communities – do not hurt or empower people; individuals do. Whilst individuals in charge of systems have been responsible for creating cultures where depersonalisation is common, what often goes unappreciated is that responsibility has also been depersonalised. In recent recessionary times, not many top managers and leaders have been heard expressing responsibility for their ill-considered actions, nor have many individuals in power positions in our country opted to feel the pain of cutbacks to the same level as the ordinary tax-payer is forced to. It is greatly concerning when those in charge of human systems do not seek the safety that will enable them to understand, accept and take responsibility for their defensive actions, which have had and continue to have devastating effects on other people's lives. In order for a more mature society to emerge, this is precisely what needs to happen. It is necessary that the rank-and-file members of human systems become conscious of their defensive responses and begin to make more mature choices and actions but it is crucial that those in charge provide the lead in this most vital human endeavour.

To conclude, there are no quick and easy remedies for human misery and no quick and easy ways to achieve mature human development. Nevertheless, there is an answer that lies within our reach – for each of us to know the self and to take responsibility for all of our behaviours. It needs to be appreciated that the road to the recovery of self and self-empowerment is difficult – even treacherous – because of the conditional and sometimes totally neglectful holding worlds we inhabit. But history has shown that it is all but impossible to extinguish the human spirit. Those who relate with others from a solid place of interiority light the way for those who are struggling.

References

Assagioli, R. (2000): *Psychosynthesis*, Amherst, MA, Synthesis Centre Publishing.

Buckley, H., Whelan, S., Carr, N., Murphy, C (2008): *Service Users' Perception of the Irish Child Protection System*, Office of the Minister for Children and Youth Affairs, Dublin.

Brizendine, L. (2007): *The Female Brain*, Broadway, New York.

Cameron, D. (2009): *The Myth of Mars and Venus*, Oxford University Press, USA.

Corry, M. and Tubridy, A. (2005): *Depression – An Emotion, Not a Disease*, Mercier Press, Cork.

Fairbairn, R. (1994) in Birtles, E. and Sharff, D., eds. *Applications and Early Contributions*. Vol. I of *From Instinct to Self: Selected Papers of W.R.D. Fairbairn*, London and Northvale, NJ: Jason Aronson.

Ferucci, P. (2004): *What We May Be*, Jeremy P. Tracher, Inc., LA.

Freud, S. (1975): Trans. Strachey, J.: *The Standard Edition of the Complete Psychological Works of Sigmund Freud*, The Hogarth Press, London.

Gardner, H. (1993): *Frames of Mind: The Theory of Multiple Intelligences*, Basic Books, New York.

Gibran, Kahlil (1923): *The Prophet*, Penguin Books, London.

Godwin, P. (2008): *When A Crocodile Eats the Sun*, Back Bay Books.

Gray, J. (2004): *Men Are From Mars, Women Are From Venus*, Harper, London.

Greenberg, Michael (2010): *Hurry Down Sunshine*, Bloomsbury Publishing, London.

Humphreys, T. (2004): *Self-Esteem, The Key To Your Child's Future*, Newleaf, Dublin.

Humphreys, T. (2004): *Leaving the Nest*, Newleaf, Dublin.

Jung, Carl (1976): *The Development of Personality, The Collected Works of C.G. Jung*, Princeton University Press, Princeton.

Lake, Frank (1979): *Studies in Constricted Confusion: Exploration of a Pre- and*

Perinatal Paradigm, The Clinical Theology Association, Birkenhead.

Mori, A. and Mori, B. (2003): *Why Men Don't Iron*, Citadel, New York.

NSRF (2004): *National Suicide Research Foundation*, Perrott Avenue, College Road, Cork.

O'Boyle, C. and Corscadden, G. (2005): RCSI Study, unpublished.

O'Donohue, John (1999): *Anam Chara*, Bantam, London.

Rogers, Carl (1961): *On Becoming a Person: A Therapist's View of Psychotherapy, Houghton and Misslin, New York.*

Shenk, David (2010): *The Genius in All of Us*, Doubleday, New York.

Sills, F. (2009): *Being and Becoming*, North Atlantic Books, CA.

Williamson, Marianne (1992): Return to Love, Harper Collins, UK.

Winnicott, D.W. (1965): *The Family and Individual Development*, Free Association Press, London

Winnicott, D.W. (1987): *Babies and Their Mothers*, Free Association Press, London.

Index